THE HEADSPACE GUIDE TO . . .

MINDFUL EATING

ABOUT THE AUTHOR

Andy Puddicombe is a meditation and mindfulness expert. An accomplished presenter and writer, Andy is the voice of all things Headspace. In his early twenties, midway through a university degree in Sports Science, Andy made the unexpected decision to travel to the Himalayas to study meditation instead. It was the beginning of a ten year journey which took him around the world, culminating with ordination as a Tibetan Buddhist monk in Northern India. His transition back to lay life in 2004 was no less extraordinary. Training briefly at Moscow State Circus, he returned to London where he completed a degree in Circus Arts with the Conservatoire of Dance and Drama, whilst drawing up the early plans for what was later to become Headspace. He has been featured widely in international press, appearing in Vogue, NYT, FT, Entrepreneur, Men's Health and Esquire, to name but a few. He also makes regular appearances on TV and online, having been featured on BBC, Dr Oz, Netflix and TED. Andy currently lives in Venice, California, with his wife Lucinda and their son Harley.

ALSO BY ANDY PUDDICOMBE

The Headspace Guide To... Mindfulness and Meditation
The Headspace Guide To... A Mindful Pregnancy

THE HEADSPACE GUIDE TO . . .

MINDFUL
EATING

Andy Puddicombe

HODDER

First published in Great Britain in 2012 by
Hodder & Stoughton
An Hachette UK company

Reissued in paperback in 2015

5

A CIP catalogue record for this title
is available from the British Library

ISBN 978 1 444 72221 5

Typeset in Celeste by Palimpsest Book Production Limited, Falkirk, Stirlingshire

Printed and bound by Clays Ltd, St Ives plc

Hodder & Stoughton policy is to use papers that are natural, renewable and recyclable products and made from wood grown in sustainable forests. The logging and manufacturing processes are expected to conform to the environmental regulations of the country of origin.

Hodder & Stoughton Ltd
Carmelite House
50 Victoria Embankment
London EC4Y 0DZ

www.hodder.co.uk

ACKNOWLEDGEMENTS

I am always touched by the support and generosity that we receive at Headspace and I'd like to thank everyone who has contributed to, assisted with, or inspired the writing of this book. In particular I'd like to thank:

Dr Judson Brewer, Neuroscientist from Yale Medical School, for his advice, support and insightful foreword;

Rich Pierson and the entire Headspace team, for their passion, encouragement and creative drive to make Headspace and *The Headspace Guide to Mindful Eating* everything it is;

Nick Begley, for his extensive scientific contributions;

Hannah Black, Kate Miles and the entire Hodder team for once again making the process of writing so enjoyable and straightforward;

Lucinda Puddicombe, Exercise Physiologist and Dietary Consultant, for her advice and expertise, but more importantly still, for agreeing to be my wife. I love you very much.

And last, but by no means least, my family, friends and the intensely loyal Headspace Community, who are a constant source of inspiration with their stories of success and who encourage me on a daily basis to make meditation and mindfulness more accessible to all.

A very big thank you to each and every one of you.

CONTENTS

A BIT ABOUT HEADSPACE

Headspace was set up in 2010 by Andy Puddicombe and Rich Pierson, to improve the health and happiness of the world through meditation practices – making them accessible, practical and relevant tools for modern-day living.

The mission of Headspace is to get as many people in the world as possible to take 10 minutes out of their day to practise a simple mindfulness-based meditation technique (included in this book), the type of which has been scientifically proven to promote a wide range of health benefits.

In fact Headspace are actively working in partnership with Yale Medical School, University College London, and many other respected universities around the world to further the understanding of meditation, and to highlight the significant impact it can have on the lives of those who practise it on a regular basis.

The broader vision of the project is to encourage people to integrate this simple yet powerful practice into everyday life. Mindful eating, the topic of this book, is just one example of how mindfulness can be applied to a very ordinary activity to achieve extraordinary results. In short, a happier, healthier and more balanced way of life.

If you'd like to join the hundreds of thousands of people already enjoying the benefits of the Headspace Take10 programme, you can sign up for it now, free of charge, at www.headspace.com or by downloading our mobile app, also called Headspace, available now for iPhone and Android.

For all other information about Headspace, the Headspace Journey, the subscription programme, events, scientific research, or the Headspace Foundation, please visit the website at www.getsomeheadspace.com

You can also follow Headspace on Facebook and Twitter and Instagram:

www.facebook.com/HeadspaceOfficial

Twitter @Andy_headspace
@Get_Headspace
Instagram @headspace

FOREWORD

Judson Brewer MD PhD
Medical Director, Yale Therapeutic Neuroscience Clinic
Yale University School of Medicine

In his new book, Andy Puddicombe has done a superb job of clearly articulating how and why eating, and indeed over-eating, has become such an issue for so many of us. At the same time, he introduces the concept of mindful eating in a practical and accessible way, demonstrating how mindfulness may well hold the key to unraveling many of these widespread problems.

In my own research I see so many of us learn to associate different moods and emotions with eating. We go out to dinner to celebrate an event, or feel depressed and eat to feel better. This pattern of behaviour becomes habitual and the next time we feel down, our brain says, 'Hey, last time you felt this way, you ate chocolate and felt better. Do it again!'. And so a spectrum of behaviours develop, ranging from comfort eating to food addiction.

Only when we can stop and notice this chain of events, can we start to change our behaviour. This is where mindfulness comes in. It teaches us to simply observe thoughts as thoughts, feelings as feelings, cravings as cravings, and nothing more. Mindfulness training gets to the heart of the problem, enabling us to change our behaviour while maintaining our sanity and happiness.

I started meditating in medical school after going through a stressful breakup. Before long I was calmer, less stressed and, by the time I completed my MD/PhD, I was meditating every day. I was so impressed with the effects of meditation that I switched my entire research career path away from studying mouse models on the effects of stress on the immune system, to studying the effects of mindfulness and meditation in humans, and how it can help them with addictions.

In a recent mindfulness study here at Yale, we found that a meditation-based approach to smoking cessation actually beat the American Lung Association program in just 4 weeks, which has long been regarded as the gold standard in the US. There were no drugs involved and it required very little time each day, with the participants simply learning the fundamentals of mind-fulness and an accompanying technique. I mention this because there are many parallels to the addiction of smoking and the current obesity epidemic.

As with food, people addicted to cigarettes habitually reach for a cigarette when under stress. This makes them feel better temporarily, but the fix doesn't last, and so the next time they get stressed, they have another cigarette, reinforcing the habit. In our study we taught people how to simply observe their thoughts, emotions, and cravings, and to notice how these led to smoking. When they could clearly see that they were driven to smoke by cravings, they were then able to observe these as sensations, rather than experiencing a compulsion to act. By observing and not acting, they were disengaging the chain, and 'unlearning' the feeling > craving > smoking association. And what we found was that the more they practiced meditation, the better they did.

The numerous studies being carried out by my laboratory, and other laboratories across the world, are starting to show that mindfulness training is an excellent tool for changing behaviour for good. The implications for how it can affect the way we shop, cook, eat and relate to the food around us is nothing short of profound.

In *The Headspace Diet*, Andy shows how food is not the problem, our relationship to it is. Where other treatments and fads focus on quick fixes, learning mindfulness can help us take a fresh look at how we've learned to eat, based on our thoughts and feelings rather than nutritional requirements. He guides us to see these clearly, helping to change our relationship to food forever, and in the process, makes mindfulness supremely palatable.

INTRODUCTION

It's just waiting there, looking at you. It knows you want it, that all it has to do is sit there long enough. It knows that you've been in this situation before, that you'll never be able to resist the temptation. The taste, the smell, that creamy sensation in your mouth and that addictive rush of sugar. Every physical sense is alive in anticipation, just waiting for the first cracks to appear in the mind, for the willpower to exhaust itself and the inevitable excuses and justifications to take hold. Sure, you could put it back in the freezer, but it's too late for that now. You'll be able to see it in your mind and hear it calling your name, even when it's safely behind closed doors.

'Eat me, just eat me – I won't tell anyone. Look, we'll make this the very last one and then from Monday you won't ever need to do it again. If you think about it, this just makes up for the time you skipped lunch the other day. Besides, I thought you'd made a resolution to be kinder to yourself, more accepting. Isn't this the perfect opportunity to be kinder to yourself, to prove that you're happy with who you are, that you don't care what other people think? And hey, once it's done, you won't have to think about me any more, right? I suppose you *could* just throw me away, but that would be wasteful, wouldn't it? You'd feel even worse, you know you would. Hardly fair on the starving children in the world, is it? Just eat me . . . '

And so the madness begins. Seriously, when did we start having conversations with our food? When did the simple act of eating become an *issue*? And how did one of the most basic and primal human needs become such an emotional minefield? Should we blame it on our parents, like everything else in life? Or should we blame it on ourselves, for not having superhuman powers of enduring will? Perhaps we should blame it on the food industry for manipulating nature to create mass-produced, highly refined foods? Or on the covers of glossy magazines, which continue to promote airbrushed, fat-free beauty as the modern standard by which are all judged?

Looking for something to blame is perfectly natural, but it serves little purpose and rarely promotes genuine change. The shape of your body, and the health of your mind, are inevitably a consequence of both nature and nurture in whatever given measure. There's no question that *all* of the factors listed above will have played a part in defining how you *see* yourself, and how you *feel* about yourself. But whilst it can be useful to understand how all these different influences affect us on such a personal level, it's important to see them in context. And that's because in order to effect *real* change, genuine and sustainable change, we need to recognise and accept that *we ourselves* are responsible for what we put in our mouths. Sure, society may not be helping us with all the conflicting messages and overly processed foods. But ultimately, we ourselves are responsible for taking good care of our health, our diet, and for feeling comfortable and at ease with who we are and what we look like.

Take a moment to think about what it would be like to no longer have that endless inner dialogue, the incessant chatter about food. Or consider what it would be like to no longer *care* about that inner dialogue, to no longer give it so much importance. What would it be like to bring a balanced but carefree attitude to your eating habits, not relying on the shaky and often unpredictable nature of willpower, but instead relying on a profound new understanding of the human mind and its limitless potential? What might it be like to have an entirely new relationship with food, to give up feelings of guilt, anxiety and craving, and instead regain that sense of healthy appreciation and enjoyment that all good food deserves? And what if that same approach showed you how to make genuinely sustainable change, towards better physical health and a body shape that left you feeling confident as well as comfortable? Welcome to *The Headspace Diet*.

MY OWN EXPERIENCE

As you've probably already realised, this is no ordinary diet book. If it were, I'd be staring out at you from the front cover, trying to look sincere and giving you my best 'You can do it!' look. Either that, or I would have paid an attractive, toned young couple to appear on the cover in very little clothing, offering you a none-too-subtle message of 'buy this book and get abs like these!' If this were an ordinary diet book, I would also be telling you that this is my very own, unique discovery, found nowhere else in the world. I might suggest that you eat nothing but a rare Himalayan berry for breakfast, lunch and dinner, every day, for the rest of your life.

Fortunately, this book is different. For starters, I'm not a doctor, nutritionist or dietician (although I have enlisted the help and expertise of these professionals in writing this book). I'm not even a celebrity – the ultimate qualification for writing a diet book. In fact I'm a former Buddhist monk and a meditation and mindfulness teacher. I'm trying to spread these practices to help people achieve a better understanding of their thoughts, emotions and behaviour. In understanding those things, in being able to see them from a new perspective, they are then able to make the changes they want to make in life, no longer held hostage to emotion, or trapped by the endless cycle of thought.

The focus of the book is, therefore, more on *how* to eat, rather than *what* to eat. But for those of you who feel a little uncertain about which foods best support positive health and wellbeing, I've included a Headspace Handy Guide to Nutrition in Chapter 10, along with a 10-Day Eating Plan to get you started in Chapter 9. I'd also suggest you give the Headspace app a try; it's the perfect compliment to the exercises in this book. You'll find it online at headspace.com or by searching 'headspace meditation' in the App Store or on Google Play.

I should say up front that when it comes to madness around food, I really do know what I'm talking about – and not just from my professional experience. Before I went away to train in mindfulness more than 18 years ago, I was obsessed with food, with eating, and most definitely with body image. And I *do* mean obsessed. I *worked* in the local gym, *trained* in the local gym; in fact I pretty much *lived* in the local gym. I competed in gymnastics whilst studying exercise, anatomy and nutrition at university. At home, I weighed out each and every portion of food that I ate. When I went out, I would either take my own food with me (picture if you will taking a Tupperware container to a restaurant), or call ahead to make sure they could cook me an egg-white omelette. At the time I could have told you the exact number of calories, grams of fat, or pretty much anything else you might have wanted to know about most foods in existence. In fact I'm not proud to say that back in those days I think I once even used the calorie count of a pint of beer as a 'chat-up line'. The fact that she was impressed makes the story sadder still.

This approach to life was deeply unfulfilling. I was tired of chasing after a mental image that always remained one step ahead of me. I was exhausted trying to maintain the size and shape I had achieved. I was confused about how others saw me (and how I saw myself). But most of all, I was bored of focusing on me and tired of the endless thoughts about what to eat and what not to eat, and tired of feeling anxious, even scared, about food. It wasn't until I went away to become a Buddhist monk that things really began to change (becoming a monk will do that). In fact it was at the monastery that I was first introduced to the technique of mindfulness.

In a world crying out for sane advice on weight loss and body image, I'm always surprised that mindful eating has not been popularised sooner in the West. After all, there's documented evidence to show that it's been around for well over two thousand years. Whilst some people have adopted mindfulness as a broader system of training the mind (as we did in the monastery), others have used it as a very deliberate strategy for maintaining a healthy relationship with food, their body image and their weight. However you choose to relate to mindful eating, I genuinely hope that in a world of fads and quick-fixes, the knowledge that it has been refined over so many years gives you a huge amount of confidence in applying this simple and easy-to-learn technique.

A BRIEF WORD ABOUT MINDFULNESS

Although mindfulness has received a huge amount of press in recent years, it's often talked about in very vague terms, and so it's not always easy to understand how it can be applied to everyday activities such as eating. Mindfulness is usually defined as being present, undistracted by thoughts and emotions, and with an attitude of mind which is neither critical nor judgemental. A bit of a mouthful, but all it really means is to live with a sense of happy contentment. This is in sharp contrast to how many people live, caught up in distracting thoughts about the past and the future, swept away by difficult emotions, and often in the habit of criticising themselves or others. This is especially true when it comes to food and the body, and many people, quite understandably, feel completely overwhelmed by these thoughts and feelings.

It's perhaps no surprise then that mindfulness has become such a hot topic within the world of neuroscientific research. Respected universities and medical institutions from around the world now regularly publish scientific papers on the benefits of mindfulness-based meditation, the conclusions of which can often be found in newspaper headlines and health columns. Whilst some researchers focus on the physical and emotional health benefits, of which there are many, others examine how mindfulness affects thought itself; how it can reduce the endless cycle of thinking, and therefore lead to a happier and more peaceful existence. More relevant to this book, however, is the exciting research that demonstrates the positive effects of mindfulness on diet, eating habits and emotional cravings (the highlights of which I've included throughout). Who wouldn't be inspired to know that by doing a simple and easy-to-learn daily mindfulness exercise, it's possible to increase activity in the part of the brain responsible for self-control and decision-making? And who wouldn't be inspired to know that in one particular study, mindfulness was shown to reduce weekly food binges by between 50 and 70 per cent?

As inspiring as these facts and figures may be, it's only when you actually *apply* the technique of mindfulness that you will see the results. It's amazing that science has made all of these discoveries, and the results of such trials can really help to motivate you when it feels as though things aren't moving as quickly as you'd like them to. But the findings only become truly valuable and relevant when they are put into practice, when they become an established part of your life and thereby a genuine cause of change. That's because, in the fullest sense, mindfulness means much more than simply being present. It also means to be curious, interested; to have a genuine desire to investigate how and why you think and feel the way you do. This means not taking *my* word for what mindfulness is, but experimenting, and finding out for *yourself*. You may find Chapter 4 especially helpful, as you begin to investigate your relationship with food and discover what type of eating personality you are.

In fact, given that we're considering the potential of giving up diets *forever*, you might like to apply this same sense of nonjudgemental investigation and curiosity to your *past* experiences of dieting as well. For example, have diets worked for you in the past? And by that I don't mean: have a few days of starving yourself enabled you to get into your favourite outfit in time for the Christmas party? I mean, has dieting enabled you to lose weight and regain your ideal shape for a sustained period of time, without becoming fanatical about food? Have diets helped you to feel better about yourself, to raise your levels of inner confidence and self-esteem? Have they enabled you to have a healthy relationship with eating, to put an end to all the inner chatter about food? The truth is, commercial diets rarely bring about this kind of change. There are so many people in the world unhappy with the way that they look, unhappy with their weight, often desperately so, and many more who spend their lives hopping from one diet to the next, looking for that miracle 'cure' – all to no avail. Being able to acknowledge these simple but often ignored truths is just one of the many gifts of mindfulness, and the very first step to changing the way you relate to food and your body.

THE 10-DAY PLAN

In following the 10-Day Mindful Eating Plan, you can, and most probably *will*, experience real, noticeable change. In some scientific trials, mindfulness has been shown to have significant benefits in as little as 5 days. However, it would be unrealistic to suggest that the attitudes, beliefs and habits of a lifetime will change in just over a week. And you'd be right to be sceptical if I suggested otherwise. It will take a bit longer than this for a more fundamental change to take place, but everything has to start somewhere. Mindfulness is a journey, and the 10-Day Plan is the beginning of that journey.

As you'll discover, mindful eating is ultimately a way of living, rather than a quick-fix plan to a temporary problem. And because it's an approach that is so subtle, so effortless, and so refined, you won't even think of it as a 'plan'. It will just be *what you do, how you live, the way you are.* And isn't that the goal for all of us? To be ourselves, happy with who we are, focused on our health, our happiness, and the wellbeing of others around us, rather than the calorie content of our next meal?

The 10-Day Plan, outlined in Chapter 9, is designed to intro- duce you to the concept of mindful eating, to get you up and running, and to ensure that you see genuine change in the way that you eat, and the way in which you relate to both food and your body. In this sense, the book contains everything that you will ever need to know to *live* mindfully and to *eat* mindfully. But when you finish the 10 days you may well still want some longer-term support. So remember to check out the Headspace website at headspace.com for additional guidance, inspiration and help.

So, let's start to enjoy food again. Let's remind the body of its own natural intelligence and its ability to self-regulate the ideal weight and shape – for you! Let's find a way to step back from all the unhealthy thinking around food and get a fresh perspective instead. Let's find a way to short-circuit those powerful emotional feelings which can feel so all-consuming. Let's find a way to be comfortable and at ease with who we are and how we look. Let's give up the endless yo-yo dieting with its short-term focus and extreme rules. Let's find a way of cultivating a sustainable, balanced and healthy approach to eating. And last, but by no means least, let's get some much needed headspace around the way we eat, the way we look, and the way we live.

CHAPTER ONE

THE FIRST THOUGHT OF FOOD

FOOD AND THE MIND

How often do you think about it? About food, that is. Seriously, on any given day, how many times do you think about food or the effect food has on your body? Not just what you want to eat, but also what you ate in the past or what you plan to eat in the future? Be sure to include the number of times you wish you *hadn't* eaten something in the past, and also what you're planning *not* to eat in the future. Now add to that every thought you ever have about your body image and the way you look. That includes every thought expressing contentment with how you look, as well as every thought in which you wished you looked different. Hard to measure, I know, but how many thoughts a day do you think that is?

Research figures vary on this question, reporting that the number of thoughts that people have about food alone can be anything up to 200 a day. Although, having done a great deal of research for this book, I suspect that figure may well be substantially higher, especially when thoughts about body image are thrown into the mix. For many, food is the first thing they think of in the morning and their body image is the last thing they think of at night. These thoughts stand like bookends at either end of the day, sandwiching feelings of craving and resistance, appreciation and discomfort, satisfaction and guilt. In fact, it's hard to imagine another topic that consumes more of our valuable headspace. Now that's not to say that there's anything inherently wrong with daydreaming about chocolate fudge cake, in fact it's quite normal. It's just that if the wandering mind is left unchecked, it can lead us down a path that we'll probably later regret. Oh, and just in case you're wondering about any other potential contender for this top spot, apparently women report thinking about food at least twice as many times as they think about sex. And whilst for men that figure is lower, food still just tops the stakes in the overall thought-count.

Over the years there's been a huge amount of public education on what foods we *should* eat and what we *shouldn't*, which foods are healthy and which foods are unhealthy. This is a good thing. This is information that everyone should possess. Admittedly, this information is often a little conflicting, and a 'superfood' hailed one week for its cancer-preventing, fertility-enhancing, fat-metabolising properties will, almost inevitably, later be dismissed for its cancer-inducing, sterility-promoting, obesity-causing qualities. But on the whole, most of us now know what we need to eat to be healthy, right? We know the rules, we know what foods promote good health and we know what foods, when consumed in excessive quantities, tend to lead towards weight-gain, obesity, hypertension and heart disease.

And yet nothing changes. The number of people who are overweight continues to rise, the number of people who are obese continues to rise, as do the number of people suffering from heart disease, diabetes, eating disorders, allergies, intolerances and everything in-between. So why is this happening and what can we do about it? The starting point is to recognise that in situations when we have freedom of choice (and there are many sections of society where this is not always the case), the food itself is not the root cause of obesity, or of being overweight. Sure, it plays an important part, but the decision of what to consume stems from our own mind. Whilst it may well be *influenced* by many contributing factors, the decision to choose 'this' food over 'that' comes from a thought, a feeling, and the willingness to engage and follow that thought or feeling.

Now this isn't an excuse to beat yourself up for the way you eat or the way you look. The mind is a powerful thing and, untrained, is a slave to both emotion and habit, which can feel so overwhelming. Remember, this isn't about blaming yourself (or anyone else). This is about trying to understand the root of the problem, so that you can create the conditions for positive change in the future. Food is simply the *object* of fascination and distraction, it is not the *cause* of it. It has no real power in and of itself; it just sits there, waiting to be eaten (or not eaten). The decision whether to eat it is ultimately yours alone. And this is important, because if the decision is *yours*, then *you* have freedom, *you* have the potential for change, the potential to be happy with who you are and how you look, at a weight that is comfortable, natural and right for you.

The processes at play in the mind are surprisingly straightforward, it's just that usually everything is happening so fast that there's not really time to take it all in. The physical action of reaching out for food and putting it in your mouth does not happen by accident. For a hand to reach out and pick up that next slice of pizza, tub of ice cream or glass of wine, it requires a signal from the brain. This signal might have been prompted by any number of thoughts, emotions, or physical sensations, and in many ways it doesn't really matter which of those it was. The important thing is that we create enough headspace and clarity to ensure that we don't necessarily follow that impulse. But, again, why does it happen in the first place? Why do we *do* what we so desperately don't want to do? And why do we so often feel powerless to resist the urge of a fleeting emotion?

MINDFULNESS AS A WAY OF LIVING

In order to answer these questions, we need to be able to observe the mind with a clear sense of awareness. We need to be able to see it, to understand it, and then fundamentally change the way in which we relate to it. That's why the practice, or technique, of mindfulness is so important in helping you to achieve a healthy relationship with food, your body, and your weight. It allows you to examine the root cause of any problem at source, and to take the appropriate action (or inaction, as the case may sometimes be), rather than waiting until you have a basket full of unhealthy food that you try to talk yourself out of buying.

As I said in the Introduction, the easiest way to think about mindfulness is to regard it as being present, in the moment, totally and wholeheartedly engaged with whatever you are doing. I'm sure you will have found yourself in that place at some time. You may even have experienced it whilst enjoying an especially good meal. The good thing about mindfulness, no matter what situation you experience it in, is that it tends to result in an absence of background chatter, not to mention a suspension of self-criticism. Although it may happen infrequently, or to happen by chance, pretty much everyone has had their own experience of it and has their own way of describing it. Whether it's a feeling of being grounded, at ease, in the moment, or even 'in the zone', it's simply another word for the same thing – the experience of the present moment.

Essentially we're talking about living in the here and now with a sense of ease. Sounds pretty nice, right? But how often do you experience that? And if you do have those moments now and then, perhaps you find them a little unpredictable. Wouldn't it be nice to be able to have that 'here and now' experience as your default setting in life? Wouldn't it be a relief to have a feeling of acceptance towards your body, together with a healthy respect and appreciation of food – and all whilst moving towards your ideal weight, size and shape?

Many people spend their entire lives lost in thought. A recent medical paper published by Harvard University reported that people's minds were wandering nearly 50 per cent of the time. Given that this was subjective feedback, it's quite likely that the figure is higher than that. Take a moment to consider how much time you spend in your head, lost in thought: 20 per cent of the day?; 50 per cent of the day?; 80 per cent of the day? When it comes to mind-wandering, there are some important implications for eating. While it's OK to daydream once in a while, if we're busy gorging ourselves whilst lost in thought, unaware of how much we are eating, and sometimes even *what* we are eating, then it is reasonable to assume that eventually we're going to find ourselves in a situation where we're not entirely happy with the way we look.

It would be tempting to race ahead and start trying to apply mindfulness to eating right away. After all, if it's mind*less*ness that causes us to make bad decisions, then clearly mind*ful*ness is going to give us the awareness to make the right decisions. But there's some important information to share with you first about practising mindfulness. Because, although it's possible to learn mindfulness whilst eating, or during any other kind of activity for that matter, it's in no way the easiest or most effective way of learning mindfulness. When it comes to being present, familiarity is everything, and the secret to that is doing a short 10-minute mindfulness-based meditation exercise each day, undisturbed and undistracted. At Headspace we call this Take 10. It's simple, easy-to-learn, and entirely manageable, even for those with the most demanding of lifestyles.

Oh, and in case you're put off by the sound of meditation and are tempted to skip the next couple of pages, you might just want to read this bit of information first. In 1994, the National Institute of Health began a research programme entitled 'The National Weight Control Registry' or 'NWCR'. It was set up to investigate and identify the common characteristics of people who successfully lose weight and keep it off. According to published research on this group, the successful participants share many common behaviours. To begin with, they eat a low-calorie, low-fat diet, and have breakfast almost every day. They also have a high level of physical activity, exercising (often walking) for almost one hour a day. So far so normal. However, what may surprise you is that 'almost everyone' who successfully lost weight and kept it off, incorporated, and I quote, 'a meditative element' into their lives. This was typically to help control stress and cravings, to enhance mood, or to improve quality of sleep: all key factors in successful weight loss. Now, as mindfulness is often described as the Rolls-Royce of meditation techniques, and Take10 is widely regarded as one of the easiest ways to learn it, the idea of doing a simple exercise like this each day starts to make a great deal of sense. In fact, given the recent discoveries about mindfulness in clinical trials, it would surely be madness not to Take10 each day.

MEDITATION AS A FORM OF SUPPORT

What picture came to mind when you read the word meditation? Was it the tree-hugger? The vegetarian? The hippy? The yoga-nut? Or maybe the shaven-headed monk sitting in a mountain retreat high in the Himalayas? These are just a few of the many ways in which meditation is often presented and viewed in the West. But things are thankfully changing, and fast. Mindfulness-based meditation has been thoroughly embraced by the medical community, approved for use by the UK National Institute for Clinical Excellence (NICE) many years ago, and is now studied by neuroscientists all over the world. It has also appeared widely across all sections of the popular media.

Although meditation *traditions* vary greatly, the one thing that can be said of pretty much all meditation techniques is that they are a subtle, yet deliberate, attempt to increase calm on the one hand and clarity on the other. Ask yourself, how much calm do you have in your life? And how much calm do you have around food? How much clarity do you have in your life? And how much clarity do you have about why you eat the way you eat? I'm assuming that you will almost certainly want to develop more of both – after all, who wouldn't want more calm and clarity in their life? Especially if the absence of one or the other (or both) is causing you to make bad choices around food.

So, rather than think of meditation as some kind of religious journey or mystical experience (unless that's your thing, of course), in this context it's useful to think of meditation as a way of providing the most conducive conditions possible for learning the technique of mindfulness, and for getting some calm and clarity into your life. The Take10 exercise will be at the very heart of your mindful eating plan, the thread that holds it all together, which I'm going to explain to you shortly. As I said before, when it comes to mindfulness, it is all about familiarity, and Take10 is the quickest and best possible way of becoming familiar with the present moment. In fact, why not try this short exercise right now to get a taste of what it means to pause and take a step back from the thoughts in the mind.

HEADSPACE EXERCISE: MINI-MEDITATION

1. Sit down in a comfortable chair, with your legs and arms uncrossed. You can rest your hands in your lap, on your legs, or on the armrests, whatever feels most comfortable. As you settle into the chair, take a few big, deep breaths, breathing in through the nose and out through the mouth. After no more than three breaths you can allow the body to return to its natural rhythm of breathing, in and out of the nose.

2. Without trying to stop the thoughts in your mind in any way, place your hand on your stomach and notice the rising and falling sensation that the body creates as it breathes. Don't try to breathe in any special way, instead just follow the natural rhythm of the breath, however it appears. Allow your focus to remain with that feeling.

3. After a while your mind will probably drift off, distracted by a passing thought. When you realise the mind has wandered, simply bring it back to the rising and falling sensation. To help maintain your focus, you can count the breaths as they pass, counting one with the rise, two with the fall, then three, then four, all the way up to ten. See if you can make it to ten without getting caught up in thought, and without focusing so intently that it feels uncomfortable. Try this a couple of times.

How was it? Did you find that your mind wandered a lot, or a little? At this stage, it really doesn't matter too much how your mind behaved, and there is no right or wrong answer. Many people find that their mind is incredibly busy with thoughts when they first try this exercise, so don't be put off if that was the case for you. When you get to Chapter 7, I'll introduce you to the Take10 exercise, and show you how you can bring your mind to a very natural place of rest quite effortlessly.

At Headspace we've helped millions of people learn how to meditate. Most had never tried anything like it before and many were unsure of their ability to do it. Before they started, most said that their minds were too busy to meditate, that they didn't have time in their day to do it, even that they were too *stressed* to meditate! But everyone I've spoken to who has made the time to sit down and try it, to take 10 minutes out each day, has said they've noticed the difference. They've said that they feel calmer, more grounded, better able to make rational decisions and to make those decisions with greater clarity. Better still, for many it is now simply part of their everyday life.

When mindfulness-based meditation is approached in the right way, truly, anyone can do it. It's not just about the technique itself, it's about understanding the processes at play in the mind, the most skilful way of relating to thoughts and feelings when they appear. But it's also about integrating that new-found sense of awareness into your everyday life, into activities, your work, your relationships with friends and family and everyone else around you. So, even if you've done lots of meditation before, please do follow the advice given later in the book and take the time to visit the Headspace website at headspace.com. It's a unique resource which will give you an even greater understanding of how to get an increased sense of calm and clarity in your life. And not just around food, but in *every* aspect of your life.

MINDFUL EATING

If mindfulness means to live in the present, and Take10 is the best and easiest way for becoming familiar with that way of being, then mindful eating can be considered the application of mindfulness towards food, body image and weight loss. But before I explain mindful eating in more detail, I'd like you to try a short exercise as it really is the best way of getting a taste for the technique.

Take a piece of chocolate, or some other food you really enjoy that you would normally struggle to eat in moderation. It can be a biscuit, a cake, some crisps, a piece of cheese, but preferably something with a strong flavour. For ease of writing I've used the example of chocolate throughout this exercise, but the instructions are the same no matter what food you've chosen. I want you to eat this chocolate as if it's the first piece of chocolate you've ever tasted – and the last piece of chocolate you'll ever have the chance to taste. In short, savour it!

HEADSPACE EXERCISE: MINDFUL EATING

1. Before you pick up the chocolate, take a couple of deep breaths, in through the nose and out through the mouth, just to allow the body and mind to settle a little. Mentally leave behind whatever you're doing for a moment or two and make sure that there is nothing to distract you – that includes music, TV or the mobile phone. It's just you and the chocolate.

2. Take a moment to consider the chocolate. Where has it come from? What's in it? Try and imagine the different ingredients in their natural growing environment and even the types of people who might have grown the cocoa beans.

3. Before you begin to eat it, pause to notice if there's a feeling of impatience, of just wanting to eat it as quickly as possible. Notice if there are feelings of pleasure and excitement, or feelings of guilt and unease about the idea of eating the chocolate.

4. Slowly unwrap the chocolate and take a good minute or so to explore it with your eyes, nose and hands. Look at it closely, smell it carefully and then touch it to see how it feels. Do the emotions change when you do this? Do some become more intense and others less intense?

5. By now you'll be more than ready to taste it. Take a small bite (or alternatively put the whole thing in your mouth), but try to resist *chewing* the chocolate. Notice how it feels in the mouth, the temperature and the texture. Also become aware of the taste – whether it's sweet, bitter, creamy, etc. Try to allow the chocolate to melt in the mouth by gently moving it around with your tongue.

6. As it melts, sit back in your chair and enjoy the moment. Remember, appreciate it, savour it and enjoy it!

How was it? You probably didn't expect to be eating chocolate as part of your 10-Day Plan but, in the right quantities, none of these foods are especially harmful. And what almost everyone says after trying this exercise, really taking the time to do it properly, is that whilst they would usually hurry down one piece after another, almost without thinking, when they apply a sense of mindfulness to the proceedings, the level of satisfaction dramatically increases. Generally speaking, this means that rather than feeling the need to continue eating, just that one piece really is enough.

Remember this is a new skill you're learning here, so don't worry if it didn't work for you in that way immediately. In fact that's the whole idea of following the 10-Day Plan or the Headspace Journey. It takes time to learn a new skill, no matter what it is, and mindful eating is no exception. But once you've learnt it, you'll have an indispensable tool for life. And don't be put off by the slow speed of eating encouraged in this particular exercise. You can apply mindful eating just as easily to a quick meal. It's just that most people tend to find it a little easier to slow things down at first. Arguably, it makes the food that much more satisfying and enjoyable too.

Did you find anything surprising about the exercise? Was it radically different from how you normally eat your food? What was it like to eat undistracted, not watching TV, checking your phone, reading a magazine, a book, or doing something on the Internet? And what was it like to eat something alone, whilst not chatting to others? Did you notice your levels of hunger? Did you notice what emotions were present? Did you notice anything about the chocolate that you've never noticed before – something about its smell, appearance or taste? Funnily enough, when some people try this exercise they don't even get as far as putting the food in their mouth, because when they look at the food more closely, they simply decide they don't want it. Even though that is not the intention of the exercise, if it stops you eating highly processed and overly refined foods, then it's probably not such a bad idea.

We've become so disconnected from our food that we walk into the supermarket and buy bags of pre-prepared salad, aesthetically pleasing fruit, sanitised cuts of meat and fish, and cans of preserved vegetables – all the foods we've been eating since our childhood. And those are considered the 'good' foods. Often we don't even know why we're buying what we're buying, it's simply habit; something we've always done. Rarely do we know where the food comes from, or the ingredients that have gone into creating the finished product. These details may not seem immediately relevant to the size of your waistline but, as you'll see later in the book, they actually play a very significant role.

So, whilst mindful eating includes the simple act of being present, undistracted, and at ease whilst eating, it is also much broader than this. Because if you trace the steps back, it's easy to see that the potential for change begins much, much earlier. It begins when you reach for the food, when you prepare the food, perhaps when you cook or shop for the food. It begins when you sit and mentally prepare the shopping list, when you make the decision to buy something based on desire, habit, or a fleeting advertisement for a special offer. This is how far we need to trace back to see those very first thoughts, the formation of the feelings that lead us to eat the things we wish we didn't eat so much of.

MAKING THE MOST OF THIS BOOK

But how are you going to make this book work for you, really work for you . . . not just for the next 10 days, but for the rest of your life? How are you going to *get* in shape, *stay* in shape, for *good*? Here are some initial invaluable tips for getting the very most out of this book.

Define Your Motivation

When it comes to making changes and sticking to them, motivation is everything. If your motivation is clear and you know exactly why you're doing something, then more often than not you'll do it. Sometimes our motivation can be a little hazy. We might have a vague idea that we want to get fit, lose weight or change the shape of our body, but we don't really have a clearly defined idea of why we're doing it, how we're going to make it happen, and what our exact goal is. Because of this, we often slip up at the very first hurdle, or find an excuse to give up as soon as a convenient obstacle arises. My hunch is that you'll find this plan so engaging that you'll have no problems at all in sticking to the practice of mindful eating. But all the same, begin this programme sure in your own mind of what you're doing, why you're doing it, what you'd like to achieve, and what you consider a realistic timeframe for making those changes. Write them down if you find that it helps.

Be Inspired

In recent years more than 2,000 scientific papers focusing on the beneficial effects of mindfulness have been peer reviewed and published in respected medical journals around the world; thousands more are waiting to be published. These studies come from respected institutions, including universities such as Yale, Harvard, Princeton, Oxford and Cambridge. In fact here at Headspace we're working directly with some of these institutions to further the understanding and benefits of mindfulness. And there's a very good reason for their interest. Mindfulness works! It has been shown to be effective in many areas of physical, emotional and mental health, and early signs show that it is just as effective in addressing the factors involved in overeating and low self-esteem. Use this knowledge to get inspired, to gain confidence in the technique you'll be applying, and to make mindful eating an integral part of everyday life.

See it Through

It sounds obvious, but you'd be amazed how many people buy a book with the intention of making changes in their life, only to read it and then place it on the bookshelf without actually applying any of the principles offered inside. And then there are those who *do* read the book, feel a little unsatisfied that they've not dropped a hundred pounds after the first couple of days and give up without seeing the programme through. And then last, but by no means least, are those people who follow the programme to the letter, experience fantastic results, and then for some inexplicable reason decide not to continue with it. This plan will only work if you try it, use it and apply a determined approach to it. It is not a diet that dictates what you eat, nor does it rely on willpower alone. This is what makes mindful eating a sustainable plan for life.

Throw Away the Scales

Mindful eating is about a way of living and a way of being. It is a way of spending *less* time focusing on your weight, and *more* time appreciating life itself. Nobody ever lost weight by standing on scales (unless they stood on them for a really long time without eating anything). When it comes to measuring body fat, scales simply don't work. They don't take into account lean muscle mass, hydration, or any of the other components that make up your bodyweight. If you truly embrace mindful eating, you will naturally find the weight that's right for you. You don't need scales to tell you when that is, because you'll see it for yourself. More importantly, you'll *feel* it for yourself. So, find a new interest, something to replace those endless hours of calorie counting and, whilst you're at it, throw out those scales too.

Find Lasting Contentment

As long as your happiness is dependent on the size of your chest, the shape of your waist, or the diameter of your rear-end, then life is going to feel very unfulfilling. That's not to say that you shouldn't feel good about yourself and the way that you look – it's great to admire your size and shape. But our size and shape can change constantly, as do all things in life, and so this kind of happiness is fleeting and unstable. This is why the mindfulness and meditation components of this approach are so important. Not only do they help to support your new eating habits, but they help you get in touch with that place of inner contentment, of underlying happiness, which is always there, no matter what shape, size or weight you might be.

Try Something Different

Feel free to hold on to all the good nutritional advice you may have had in the past, but right now let go of any ideas you might have about quick-fix diets and miracle makeovers. If they truly worked, they would have worked for you long before now, and the diet industry would not continue to be so successful. Yo-yo dieting is no way to live life, and neither is counting every calorie on your plate. So forget this old way of thinking and instead look to find your ideal weight through a new, *healthy* relationship with food. Remember, mindful eating is not so much about *what* you eat or the *quantity* consumed (although they're both very important factors), it's more about *how* you eat, your *relationship* with food, and how that *influences* your diet.

Forget Blame

All of us can find excuses for why we are the way we are, why we look the way we look, or why we eat the way we eat. Blame is easy, whether it's directed towards oneself or others. But nothing productive comes from blame. You don't get to change the shape of your body or reach your ideal weight by blaming others. Blame simply encourages a negative pattern of thought, which keeps you stuck exactly where you are. So make a deal with yourself, no matter what has been done or not done in the past, no matter what has been said or left unsaid in the past, and no matter what thoughts you've had or not had in the past, let them go and leave them behind where they belong – in the past. That's the beauty of meditation: it shows you how to let go of these things. Mindful eating, and mindfulness in general, will show you that you have the freedom to be exactly who you want to be, without being attached to old ways of thinking and the futile blame game that sabotages so many attempts at weight loss.

Accept You Can Change

Sometimes emotional patterns can feel so ingrained that it's hard to imagine that they are not part of who we are. It can be tempting then to throw in the towel before we've even started, to think 'what's the point?'. But doing that is to deny a simple fact of life. Every*thing* and every*one* is always changing. Science has shown how after just five days of practising an easy-to-learn mindfulness-based meditation technique, the area of the brain associated with self-control becomes more active. Even more impressively, after a total of 11 hours that same part of the brain is starting to show *physical* changes in its structure. This is what it means to rewire the brain, to unlearn old habits. It's not just about thinking in a different way, it's about providing the right conditions for fundamental changes to your hard drive.

Listen to Your Natural Intelligence

There is nothing in nature more incredible than the human body. Its ability to adapt, to change and to survive is extraordinary. And yet we somehow feel the need to interfere with its regulation. Rather than making our food choices based on hunger, we make them based on emotion and the image we have of ourselves. But the body knows what it's doing and knows what it needs to do to be at its optimum weight and size; we just need to know how to listen to it, which feelings we need to respond to and which feelings we need to let go of. This is what mindfulness is all about – the ability to listen, to learn and to trust in the natural intelligence of both body and mind. Mindful eating shows you how.

Get Physical

Although mindful eating will help you to lose weight, without any physical exercise it's unlikely to help you to drastically change the shape of your body. Engaging the body in some form of physical exercise is unquestionably good for you – but then you probably knew that already. You don't need to become a gym bunny; it can be as simple as taking a good brisk walk each day, with some simple bodyweight exercises for further toning. But whatever you decide to do, you need to do it *regularly* if it is going to make a difference. When you exercise wonderful things begin to happen in the body. Not only do you start to burn body fat, but your metabolism is increased, your blood flow and circulation is improved, powerful chemicals are released bringing about a feeling of energy and wellbeing, and very often feelings of tension and stress simply melt away. So do your body a favour, and try and get some physical exercise each day.

Avoid Comparison

In many ways we are all remarkably similar as human beings. At the same time, each and every one of us is undeniably unique: our genetic code is slightly different from that of the person next door, our upbringing is likely to be different from that of the person working across the street, and our day-to-day life is likely to be radically different from those of the sleek, chiselled and toned models smiling at us brightly from the front of glossy magazines. Remember, mindful eating is not about finding *somebody else*'s ideal weight and size, it's about *you* finding your *own* ideal shape and size.

Take10 Each Day

You may not have come across meditation as part of an approach to food and diet before, but don't underestimate its importance as part of this plan. Remember, meditation provides the perfect conditions for learning how to be mindful, and mindfulness is the key to the success of this entire approach. If you can learn how to cultivate a strong sense of awareness while sitting quietly, undisturbed, for a short period of time each day, then you will have no problem at all in applying that same sense of calm and clarity to your eating habits. You'll find all the details you need for Take10 in Chapter 7. (Some of you might prefer to be led through the exercise as a guided meditation and you can do this via the Headspace website or via the headspace app.) Even if you only do the exercise for the 10 days of the programme, it will give you a unique insight into your own mind, of how and why you think and feel the way you do.

Live Life Mindfully

Our mind is with us wherever we go. When you learn mindfulness for one area, you learn mindfulness for all areas. In developing the ability to be aware, to have a sense of calm and clarity around food and your eating habits, you develop the potential to apply those qualities to every aspect of your life at the same time. So, don't be surprised if mindfulness starts to have a positive influence on other areas of your life as well. It's quite normal to experience a greater sense of calm in situations where you might usually feel anxiety. It's not uncommon to find relationships running more smoothly as you become more patient and understanding of others. And it's quite usual to have greater clarity about important life decisions – food-related or otherwise.

Think More About Others

For most people, getting fit, eating well, and even losing weight requires a lot of self-interest. Very often they become addicted to this way of thinking, this way of being, their life revolving around an obsessive or fanatical interest in their shape, size and weight. It is not a fun way to live, either for the individual or for those around them. So, it can be useful to take a step back now and then and see how these changes affect others around you, as well as yourself. Perhaps your motivation for getting in shape could be to stay fit and healthy for your children, for your parents and the other people close to you in your life. After all, this isn't simply about looking nice on the outside, it's also about staying healthy on the inside. Most people find that when they flip their motivation to make it more about others, life not only feels more comfortable, but those pesky, often hard-to-reach goals feel that much easier to achieve.

Use the Headspace Website

www.headspace.com

Remember, although this book has everything in it that you'll need to begin your journey of mindful living and mindful eating, the Headspace website will undoubtedly add to your experience. On the site you'll find animations, videos and audio tracks that help to make meditation easy to understand and mindful eating easy to apply. So, look out for the links to the useful pages on the Headspace website throughout this book. And, if you start to notice the difference in the way you look and feel over the next 10 days, and decide that you'd like more support and advice, or even that you'd like to sign up to the Headspace Journey for a year-long plan of mindfulness-based meditation, then you can find all the information you'll need at www.headspace.com

CHAPTER TWO

THE BIG (FAT) PICTURE

A WORLD GONE MAD

In trying to understand your own relationship with food, it can be useful to take a broader view. We live in a world in which more than 1.5 billion people are considered overweight or obese, which means that almost 25 per cent of all the people in the world are posing a direct threat to their health and wellbeing through their excessive weight. That's 1 in 4 people who are at direct risk of heart disease, diabetes, high blood pressure, cancer and osteoarthritis. This is the same world in which an estimated 800 million people go hungry every day. So, there are now twice as many people in the world facing health risks due to overeating or lack of exercise, as there are people facing starvation and malnutrition through lack of food and adequate nutrients.

In Britain alone, the level of obesity has tripled in the last 20 years, with more than 60 per cent of adults now considered overweight or obese. And the news isn't much better for the younger generation either. Over the past 10 years, obesity has doubled amongst 6 year olds and tripled amongst 15 year olds.

And the forecast for the future is no better. In a recent international study led by Oxford University, it was predicted that almost half of all men and women in the UK could be obese by 2030. This massive jump is likely to have serious implications for the rest of society, not least for the healthcare services. The report suggests that it will cause an extra 668,000 cases of diabetes, 461,000 of heart disease, and 130,000 more cases of cancer. This is estimated at costing the NHS at least £2 billion extra a year. These numbers are so vast that it can be hard to relate to them. Sometimes it's easier to simply reflect on how unhappy it makes you to feel overweight, or how worried or sad you might feel at seeing a loved one suffer from the effects of being overweight or obese. When you do that, all of a sudden those numbers appear a lot more significant.

One of the shocking things about these figures is that these statistics come from predominantly developed countries. They come from societies in which wide-ranging educational policies targeted specifically at reducing obesity (and increasing the consumption of healthy foods) have been in place for many years. On the whole, these are not people who are uneducated or who don't know what they should or shouldn't be eating. And yet the problem has reached epidemic proportions and continues to rise at an alarming rate. So what's happened? What's gone wrong? Why are we getting bigger?

There's no question that as much as we are told to eat less food, eat more healthily and do more exercise by the government and other health agencies, we are at the same time encouraged to eat *more* food, eat *less* healthily, and do *less* physical exercise by an industry that relies on us to buy its products. Without wanting to sound cynical or conspiratorial in any way, it's useful to acknowledge the simple fact that certain elements of the food industry make their money, big money, huge money, from trying to sell us the same foods that we try so hard to resist.

This is a trillion-dollar industry, one of the biggest in the world. And we should be under no illusions about the primary motivation of these elements within the food industry. They are, after all, in business to make money. If they can sell us more products by refining the way things taste (read: adding more fat, salt and sugar), then we should fully expect them to do so. It doesn't make it right, but we should expect it nonetheless. Should we try and change this state of affairs? Absolutely, but that will take time. In the meantime, should we leave our food choices to the tactical recommendations and seductive advertising campaigns of the food industry? Absolutely not.

What's often overlooked is that the *diet* industry is actually part of the *food* industry and, despite the recent recession, it continues to grow at over 10 per cent a year. In fact, current predictions are that, by 2014, the global weight-loss industry will be worth an estimated $586.3 billion a year. Now I've looked at that figure over and over again. At first I thought it was a mistake. But it's not, it's really not. That's $586.3 billion spent on weight-loss foods, drinks, aids and supplements. And close to 90 per cent of this spending will come from the US and the EU alone.

Once again, just to put that figure in perspective, the United Nations has estimated the cost of ending world hunger is $195 billion a year. So, by 2014, we'll be spending almost three times as much on weight-loss products as it would cost to feed every single hungry person in the world. Can this really be considered a mindful way to eat? Can this really be considered a mindful way to *live*? Truly, it is a world gone mad. But that doesn't mean we have to be part of the madness. We can choose to make a difference, to be more mindful in the way we shop, cook, prepare and eat our food. We can choose to be more mindful in the restaurants we choose and the food that we eat when on the move. In making these choices, we not only improve our own lives and achieve our own aims, but we also begin to change the lives of others as well.

THE WORLD OF WEIGHT LOSS

Have you ever taken a really good look at the world of weight loss? Not in those guilt-ridden moments immediately after a huge dinner when you would buy anything on offer, but in those rational moments when you are simply looking to see what's around? I had one of those moments when I began the research for this book. Now I won't pretend it was entirely unfamiliar territory, because as I said earlier, before I was introduced to mindful eating I was an early adopter of many of these products. In fact I didn't just dip my toe in the water of the fat-burning industry, I ripped off my clothes and dived in head first! I bought books, magazines, foods, drinks and anything else on offer. But looking around now, I see that certain aspects of the diet industry have changed. There's now surgery and prescription medication, much of it available over the Internet. There are people out there ready and willing to reduce the length of your digestive tract, to wrap a band around your insides to limit the amount of food you can consume, or to surgically place a balloon full of water in your stomach so that you can feel fuller. There are even pills to prevent the absorption of fat into the bloodstream. This is serious stuff, undoubtedly warranted in the most chronic and acute cases, but open to abuse and misunderstanding by the wider population. Thankfully, most people will never need to resort to such drastic measures.

But what about the average person, a little overweight and wanting to shed a few pounds? Well, the wide variety of diet books that used to exist are certainly ever-present. There are the one's that encourage you to eliminate carbohydrate and eat nothing but protein, radically reducing the animal population of the world one meal at a time. And then at the other end of the scale there are those which encourage a vegan way of life, in which even dairy products are considered taboo. There are diets which promote citrus fruits to get you ready for the beach, and diets which promote high fibre vegetables to get you ready for the toilet. Many diets advocate a complete absence of solid food altogether, where all nutrients are consumed via so-called 'health shakes', usually with very scientific sounding names and containing ingredients which would appear more at home in a chemistry lab.

Seriously, you really couldn't make it up. There is a diet out there aimed at every conceivable type of person, and containing nutritional advice that often borders on the extreme. There are even hundreds of diet books aimed specifically at children and teenagers.

But whether it's books, pills, potions or lotions, many of the claims made by the manufacturers of these weight-loss products are nothing short of absurd. Some push the boundaries of science and physiology, others push the boundaries of sheer fantasy. At best, these claims are harmless, laughable even, but at worst they cause people financial stress, emotional worry and, in extreme cases, physical harm. A few years back, the Federal Trade Commission in the US published a study in which it reported that over 55 per cent of all weight-loss claims 'strained credibility'. Whilst I admire the diplomatic language, I can think of many other ways of describing these assertions.

A recent survey, by analysis group Mintel, found that approximately 13 million people in the UK are permanently on a diet. That's 1 in 4 people trying to restrict their calorie intake at any one time. The research also found that although people were conscious of the need to eat well for the sake of their health, the majority were dieting for aesthetic reasons, to look good. And this is an increasingly common trend. Is it any wonder that the weight-loss industry is worth so much money?

Now whilst I'm sure many books and diet programmes are of the highest quality and have made a difference to the lives of many, I do have serious doubts as to their long-term impact. That's because we know that these types of diets tend to be faddish and the results short-lived. Unlike mindful eating, I struggle to imagine any of these diets being around in 2,000 or 3,000 years' time (although I'm more than happy to be proved wrong). How many diets have you been on? Make a list if necessary. Of those, how many have enabled you to lose weight? Of those, how many have enabled you to reach your *ideal* weight? And of those, how many have enabled you to *remain* at that ideal weight? Exactly.

The National Institute of Health estimates that most dieters can expect to 'regain two-thirds of their lost weight within a year of completing their diet plan'. These same dieters can expect to regain 'all of their weight or possibly more within five years'. Having spoken to many men and women during the research for this book, I'm inclined to think that the figures from the NIH sound wildly optimistic. Most people I spoke to said that they rarely kept the weight off for more than a few weeks after finishing a diet. And this is the problem, diets are intended to start and then finish. It suggests something temporary. But how can something temporary be sustainable, how can something that is designed to be a short-lived experience be a lifelong way of living? And that's where mindful eating is so different. Yes, it's about a way of eating, but it's also about a way of living, a way of being – for the rest of your life. It's a way of *getting* in shape, *staying* in shape, *for life*.

THE VALUES OF SOCIETY

Why do you want to lose weight? Why do you want to change your shape, or look differently from the way you do right now? Is it for your health, because you've been told you *need* to lose weight? Or is it because you don't like the way you look or feel? Is it because one of your friends has just lost weight, because you're going on holiday soon, or because you're feeling inspired by a picture in a magazine or a story from a makeover TV programme? Take a few minutes to be clear in your own mind about why you are going to follow this 10-Day Plan, this new way of eating. Or perhaps you've no wish to lose any weight at all, but are simply looking to improve your eating habits and change your relationship with food. Either way, try and be clear about your goal. What's the most powerful influence driving that goal? And what's going to happen when you reach that goal?

These are really important questions for getting you to where you want to be with your health, weight, size and shape. It's natural to want to improve yourself, to feel your best; these are good, positive changes. But it's also important to remember that those things are only a very small part of what makes you who you are. These things do not *define* you, no matter how much it may feel that way sometimes, and no matter how many images in society might encourage you to think otherwise. For mindful eating to work, for it to become a part of how you eat and how you live for the rest of your life, it is essential that these two things are not confused. *Who you are is not how you look.* Neither is it how much you weigh, the size of your waist, or the size of your chest. That's why it's so important to find that underlying place of contentment *at the same time* as losing weight.

It's human nature to want to believe in something and for that belief to be reflected in our values. Whether we believe in an idea, a person, a concept, a method, a way of living or a way of being, we all believe in something – even if it's nothing! In general, these beliefs, values and ambitions tend to reflect those of wider society, and this has always been the case. No matter how outlandish, superficial or ill-advised, as long as enough people in society (or at least the key decision-makers and influencers) go along with it, then it will become normal, acceptable, and even desirable. For example, there was once a time when being overweight was considered all the rage. It was a sign of virility, fertility, power and wealth, for both men and women alike. In fact there are still a few cultures in the world in which this attitude is upheld. But what happens when these values start to become confused? What happens when the ambitions of society no longer reflect the true wishes of the individual?

And what happens when these beliefs and ambitions begin to cause harm to society?

Most people I know just want to be happy. When it comes down to it, they just want to be at ease with themselves and feel comfortable in their own skin. The desire to get thinner or to become more toned does not come from their own personal ambition, but from a broader vision of society that encourages such behaviour. Likewise, their participation in a diet industry that promotes an endless cycle of on-again/off-again fads and fashions does not come from their own personal belief in the power of diets to deliver happiness, but from a feeling of pressure and coercion to 'keep up with everyone else'. Imagine you lived on a desert island and nobody was ever going to see you again. Would you still have the same ambitions for weight loss, the same desire to change your shape? I suspect the intensity of feeling might differ somewhat.

Taking steps to achieve your ideal weight is undoubtedly a positive course of action. But we need to make sure that the changes we make come from the right place. If they come from a place of obligation, pressure, or influence, then they are unlikely to work. Because at some stage you will want to rebel against that feeling of obligation, and we all know what happens in those situations (clear a pathway to the biscuit jar). So make sure that your motivation for this programme reflects your *own* values and not just those of wider society. We all know that the modern standard of weight, shape, size and tone, promoted on the front of every magazine, is largely unachievable – even for the most diligent and conscientious of dieters. Ironically, it is even unachievable for the typical model as well, which is why their photo will have been airbrushed so thoroughly. Those pictures have become nothing more than fantasy, computer images for us to aspire to.

But we are not computer images, and of course there *is* no airbrushing in real life. We're human beings, and our weight, shape and size should reflect this simple fact. That doesn't mean we can't look amazing, fantastic, beautiful or handsome. It doesn't mean that we shouldn't aspire to look our very best. It just means that we need the result to come from our *own* ideal vision and not some vision that society imposes upon us. So, have in mind what *you* would like to achieve from mindful eating, what weight *you* would be happy with, and what shape would help *you* to feel amazing.

YOU AND YOUR BODY

How do you feel about your body? Be brutally honest – you don't have to share this with anyone else. How does that make you feel? I realise that this may feel like torture for some people, and you shouldn't be surprised if this type of questioning brings a bit of emotion or discomfort to the surface of the mind. If that does happen, try to allow it to remain for a few minutes rather than looking for a distraction. As counter-intuitive as that may sound, this is a key aspect of mindfulness and is something that will start to make a lot more sense as you read on through the book.

When you next get a chance, I'd like you to stand naked in front of a mirror (but please, read the rest of the sentence before removing your clothes) in a private place, in your own home, where you know you won't be disturbed by anyone else. Look at yourself in the mirror. *Really* look at yourself. And now do it without holding in your stomach, inflating your chest, pouting your lips or raising your jaw-line. How does it feel? Is there calm or chaos in the mind right now? Is there clarity or confusion? Without trying to change the way you feel, without trying to create a story about the way you look, and without trying to push away any thoughts that you find uncomfortable, simply look at what you see, and *notice* how you feel. Be aware of the mind automatically zooming in on those areas which you are uncomfortable with, and as much as possible try and see the entire image, the whole body, rather than staring at any one particular part.

If you're like most people, you will have found both of those exercises a little uncomfortable. That's because reality often *is* a little uncomfortable. I don't mean the *idea* of how we look, which we carry in our mind and then project onto the image we see in the mirror. And I don't mean the idea we have of ourselves based on what others have said (or not said) to us in the past. I mean the reality – that raw, often uncomfortable place of accepting yourself exactly as you are. This is what's known as starting where you are. Because no matter how difficult this is to acknowledge and accept, the reality has to be seen clearly to affect positive change. Otherwise any changes you make will be based on confusion, a false idea of how you look. In order to create a sustainable change, there needs to be an acceptance, an understanding, of where you are right now.

Many people have such a strong vision of what they'd like to look like that they struggle greatly with accepting themselves as they are. This is common and is something which mindfulness can really help with. Many other people actually *fear* acceptance, because they think it will prevent them from reaching their weight-loss goals and ambitions. But that's to misunderstand the word. Acceptance doesn't mean to sit back and do nothing, to be indifferent to a situation that can be changed for the better. Acceptance means to acknowledge the situation as it is, to see the need for change when necessary and, where appropriate, to make those changes from a place of quiet calm and clear perception. Far too often the motivation for change comes from confusion and disquiet, from anxiety, sadness, frustration, self-hatred, loneliness or guilt. Think about it, how often have those emotions been responsible for you wanting to make changes in yourself?

Now think about what that means, the implications of that. In this situation you are left with a hopeless choice. You either have to maintain that negative feeling, that emotion, to see you through to your desired goal, or, if it really is your only source of motivation, you have to let go of the emotion and accept failure in your efforts to change.

This is tragic, and yet it is the relationship countless people have with their bodies. It means there are millions of people out there actively cultivating a sense of self-loathing and anxiety (consciously or otherwise) in order to achieve the goal of weight loss. But when they reach that goal (*if* they reach that goal), the emotion has usually become such a strong habit that they are unable to let go of it. They then become trapped in this emotional loop of hating themselves, of wanting to be different, of trying to reach perfection (whatever that is). For the others, those who are unable to sustain the prolonged attack on themselves, those who give up the emotion before reaching their goal, the confusion is compounded because they are left feeling like a failure through no fault of their own. Does any of this sound familiar? If it does, then you're by no means alone.

44

Let's get this in context. Can you change the way you look? Yes, absolutely. With the right foods, the right amount of physical exercise and a mindful approach to your eating habits, you really can change your shape, your size and your weight – for good. And this book will show you how. But don't underestimate the importance of a calm mind and a clear perspective in making these changes a reality. As strange and counter-intuitive as it may sound, accepting yourself as you look right now is what will allow you to create the right conditions for change in the future. Remember, acceptance doesn't mean a place of no change, it means change from the right place. And even when you *do* change, that doesn't change *who you are*, it changes *how you look*. And for me, that's the real beauty of mindfulness. It shows you how to find this place of quiet acceptance within yourself, a place free from thought, from judgement, criticism or blame. It shows you how to access that place of absolute peace, where self-worth, self-esteem and inner confidence come as standard, no matter what you look like and how much you weigh.

Why wait until you reach your ideal weight and body shape to be happy? Why not learn to find that underlying sense of contentment *at the same time* as reaching your weight-loss goals? That way, you can make sure that you are always approaching your goals from a good place, with a healthy and well-defined motivation. It also means that it won't take a monumental effort, putting everything else on hold, keeping all the so-called negative feelings at bay. Instead, you can go about reaching your goals in a relaxed and balanced way, living and enjoying life at the same time. Doesn't that sound like a refreshingly sane way to find your ideal weight?

YOU AND YOUR FOOD

Do you know anyone who has an entirely healthy relationship with food? I mean someone who *doesn't* experience cravings, who *doesn't* get apprehensive about eating certain foods, and who *doesn't* eat from a place of emotion rather than hunger? Do you know anyone who *never* eats food with the sole intention of losing weight, who *never* feels guilty after eating, and who's *never* overwhelmed with food-related thoughts and conflicting emotions about what they 'should' and 'shouldn't' eat?

I wish I could say I knew lots of people who have a healthy relationship with food, but the truth is, I'm struggling to name even a few. Of course, we're all on a sliding scale, but it's important to realise that you are not alone, that experiencing these difficult thoughts and feelings towards food is entirely normal, albeit with differing levels of intensity. Living in a modern society, with the values that are encouraged and promoted as 'normal', it would be almost impossible not to experience any of these thoughts or feelings once in a while.

In many ways our relationship with food is unlike any other, because we can't break this type of relationship off. There is no way of running away from yourself, or from food, and unless you're planning to head off to live in the Amazonian rainforest or the Himalayan highlands, there is no way of removing yourself from the values and attitudes of modern-day society either. So we need to find a way to have a healthy relationship with food, living in the world we inhabit, despite the pressures that exist. The starting place for that is in the here and now. Understanding how you view food *now* is essential to making changes for the *future*. For example, do you see food as a friend or an enemy? Is it something to enjoy or something to resist? Does it cause you pleasure or pain? Do you see food for what it is, or for the effect you think it will have on your weight? Do you view food as a gift, or simply as more fuel for the body? And do you have a sense of appreciation around food, or a sense of resentment?

Take a pen and paper and write down the first 10 words that come to mind when you think about food. Now think of a food you consider healthy or 'good', and write down the first three words that come to mind for that. Now repeat the exercise, but whilst thinking about a food you consider unhealthy or 'bad'. It can be surprising to see the language we use around food – sometimes we might even surprise ourselves with how strongly we feel. Recently I asked a patient who comes along to the Headspace Clinic to carry out this task. The words on the first list included associations as varied and strong as 'friends, mum, love, greed, cake, fat'. When they were asked to think of a healthy food, they came up with 'clean, happy, good' and yet when they thought of an unhealthy food, they came up with 'grease, fat, miserable'.

This is where mindfulness and mindful eating become so relevant. Because if these are the kind of thoughts going around in the mind, then it would be very easy to *react* to those thoughts, to buy into them or to argue against them, and to have even greater conflict in the mind. Mindfulness shows you how to be aware of the thoughts and feelings that exist in your mind, *free* from judgement and criticism. So, rather than *reacting* to those thoughts and feelings (continuing the usual food-related commentary or inner conflict), you are able to step back, see those feelings in a new light and *respond* from a place of calm and considered choice. This is something that can only happen when you are present and in the moment. If you are caught up in lots of distracting thoughts, of which you are not fully conscious, then it is impossible to make this distinction.

Now take a moment to consider how often you actually *taste* the food that you eat. Sure, you'll taste the first bite, at least in part because you'll want to check that you are eating what you were expecting to eat. You'll also want to check that the food is safe to eat, that it hasn't gone off. But then you'll probably quickly slip into a semi-conscious state of eating soon after. Sound familiar? I don't mean that you are half asleep or slumped on the table, but rather that you will have become involved in some other activity. It's not hard to move a fork back and forwards from a plate, or a sandwich from hand to mouth, and you will undoubtedly have developed the ability to carry out the task without even thinking about it, in much the same way as you are able to walk or breathe without conscious effort. This means we can eat our food while reading the newspaper, working on the computer, watching telly, chatting on the phone, or mentally working through our plans for the next day. And all the while we keep shovelling the food into our mouths, with just enough awareness to ensure that we don't spill it down our front.

Quite some achievement, but what it means is that we miss the *experience* of food. We eat and continue to eat when we're no longer hungry. We reach for food out of habit rather than choice. We eat with the rhythm of the activity (ever tried eating whilst watching sport or an action movie on TV?). We eat with no sense of appreciation, missing the tastes, the smells and textures of food. And then we wake up again to find it's the last mouthful. To be present for only the first and last mouthful like this is quite common.

Mindfulness (and mindful eating more specifically) will show you how to step out of this madness, how to be present, aware and skilful with the food choices you make. It will give you the ability and confidence to listen to the genuine needs of your body, rather than simply reacting to fleeting emotions. This is the foundation for any sustainable change in our eating habits and is at the very heart of mindful eating.

CHAPTER THREE

WHY WE EAT THE WAY WE EAT

There is a clear distinction to be made between *understanding* why you eat as you do, and looking for someone or something to *blame* for your current relationship with food. Understanding the cause of something (without getting too caught up in analysis of it) generally leads to greater peace of mind and a gentler acceptance of the situation as it is. Blame, on the other hand, tends to lead to *less* peace of mind and a greater amount of inner turmoil and conflict. As I mentioned earlier on in the Introduction, acceptance is often misunderstood as a very passive quality, which is somehow opposed to change. But in truth, acceptance allows you to make change from the right place, with the right motivation, and with enough clarity to make that change last. Accepting where you are right now is no different from knowing exactly where you are on a map when you set out on a journey. It's essential. Part of moving towards this place of acceptance is understanding and coming to terms with some of the many factors that may have negatively influenced your relationship with food, or indeed the way in which you relate to your body. Remember, this isn't about blame, it's about understanding.

NATURE VERSUS NURTURE

Each and every one of us is unique, an individual character with specific traits. You can see these in babies as young as just a few days old. Whilst some are naturally quiet, seemingly happy to just lie there and sleep, others are restless and noisy from the very beginning. For these very young babies, there has been no time for parental or societal influence to take effect, so character traits are usually put down to the diversity of nature. In adults you'll often see these characteristic features play out in much more obvious ways, with a very definite impact on eating habits and diet. You may well find yourself wishing that your qualities were different, that things would be so much easier if you were more like so and so. But wanting that fundamental nature to be different is not unlike wanting a green apple to be red, or a carrot to be a piece of cake.

The basic character we're born with is then overlaid with a personality that forms as we grow. This personality is infused with the values, opinions, preferences and behaviour of those around us at that early age. Whether it's our parents, siblings, extended family or other influences, all help to form our personality. This happens very early – many psychologists believe that the personality is pretty much fully formed by the age of just five or six. During this time, many of our early attitudes towards food will also have been founded. By then we would have picked up on the way food was spoken about, noticed the way in which food was consumed, how it was used to reward and to punish, and we would have realised what was considered acceptable behaviour around food, and what was considered unacceptable.

That's not to say that *all* of your eating habits will stem from that time, because many will have been formed considerably later, but it's helpful to recognise that many of your thoughts and much of your behaviour, in relation to food, will go back a long way. That's why sustainable change can never happen from a temporary diet; it takes time to rewire those established patterns of behaviour. Along the way, many people find that once they begin the practice of mindful eating, they become more aware of the origin of their eating habits. As long as this is acknowledged from a place of understanding rather than a place of blame, then this can be really useful. It may also surprise you, as you realise time and time again, 'Oh, so *that's* why I do that . . .'

THE GENETIC CODE

'It's just the way I'm built. I've always been this shape. I'm big-boned. It's in the family genes, what can I do?' How many times have you heard people say these things? Perhaps you've even said them yourself. There's no question that some people seem to have a greater propensity for putting on weight. Extensive scientific research over the years has shown that whilst some people find it very difficult to put weight *on* (try not to be too jealous), others find it difficult to take weight *off*. It's also true that some people come from families who are of – how shall we say? – hardier stock. These families are genuinely larger in frame and often stronger in nature. In the past this would have been seen as a considerable advantage, but I appreciate that will come as little comfort to those of you who wish to be lighter, smaller or thinner, and who no longer roam free with wild animals.

Is the answer to our ever-expanding waistlines therefore locked away in the genetic code of our DNA? Scientists say that the jury is still out on this one. Whilst there have been some significant findings in genetic research, it is simply too early to say whether it is the direct cause of individuals being overweight or obese. However, what they *have* concluded from their research is that in the future it will be entirely possible to manipulate these genes to reduce the likelihood of weight gain and obesity. What's less understood are the implications of tinkering with a complex chain of DNA that has happily seen us through tens of millions of years of evolution. Although, just in case you're wondering, this kind of genetic engineering is still a very long way off, so close the fridge door and don't stop reading just yet.

The idea that our weight, shape and frame are dictated solely by genetics is a popular one. After all, if this is the case and the code is firmly locked, then it gives people free rein to do what they like and to eat what they like. If they have already decided that change is impossible, then that's exactly what change will be. This attitude is often confused with acceptance, but of course it is actually something quite different and can drastically limit the potential for change. Because this is not acceptance in the objective sense of the word, where change is still possible. Instead it is a self-defeating, subjective acceptance, perhaps better characterised as 'giving up'. You can't change the basic frame of your body, but that's not to say you can't still find your own ideal weight, together with a healthy sense of appreciation and respect for your body.

PRAISE AND PUNISHMENT

How many times have you eaten something unhealthy (but nonetheless delicious), because you've told yourself you 'deserve' it, or to 'treat' yourself? Perhaps it's because you've done a good job at work, had a tough day with the kids at home, or perhaps it's because you've gone a few days or weeks following the latest diet craze (oh, the irony). Do you remember the first time you ever did this? Or, perhaps more likely, the first time this was ever 'done to you'? The first time that food was used as a reward for having done something well, or as a form of encouragement (read: bribe) for agreeing to behave well in a situation? As a parent, there is often little to work with when it comes to motivating your children to behave in a certain way, and so it's understandable that food is often used to control behaviour. It can be a way of subduing an angry child, cheering them up when sad, or giving them something to 'do' when bored. The use of food here is not a sinister method of manipulating behaviour, but a subtle way of cultivating positive social attitudes. And, as anyone with a child will tell you, there are times when a sweet in your pocket can be a lifesaver.

But what about the reverse? Were you ever *not* allowed certain foods? Were you ever told that you *couldn't* eat something that you liked, or were made to eat something that you didn't like as a form of punishment? Perhaps you were made to sit and finish your food because you'd behaved badly at the meal table (been there, done that), or because (the ultimate guilt trip for a five year old), there were 'starving children in the world'. And what about now? Do you sometimes use food as a form of punishment in your own life? Do you 'not allow' yourself certain foods when you've been 'bad' with your diet? Do you 'make yourself' eat certain foods because you think that's what you need? These behaviours run deep.

And it doesn't take a psychiatrist to see that the implications of linking food so closely to behaviour will inevitably have some lasting impact on the way we eat and the way in which we feel about ourselves. All the more so because these parental actions are very often carried out just when the personality of the child is being formed. This is when conditioned behaviours are being learnt, and behavioural responses are being experimented with. The temptation is to try and *break* the habits that were formed early on, to *resist* the urge to act in that same way, or to *convince* ourselves that we should behave differently. 'Break', 'convince', 'resist'. Hardly sounds like a recipe for peace of mind, does it? If ever there was a model for inner conflict and dwelling obsessively on food, there it is right there.

Think about it, the mind that is saying 'I must' is the same mind that's saying 'I mustn't'. There is only one mind, not two. So, how could that situation ever end peacefully? Apart from the sheer madness of arguing with oneself, one side has to win and one side has to lose. This means one part of you has to be rejected, ignored or suppressed, while the other part gets to feel very good about itself. However, what happens more often is that neither side ever really wins and there is just a lot of internal argument about which is right and which is wrong.

This is why mindful eating is so unique. It doesn't rely on self-talk, positive thinking, or shouting down the little voice that won't go away. Instead, it shows you how to step back from both the 'must' and the 'mustn't', in equal measure, allowing you to see clearly the dynamics at play in the mind. And in seeing the mind in this way, it's as if you are a *witness* to the feelings that are experienced, rather than a *hostage* to them. It's as though you have the capacity to respond from a place of skilful intention, rather than reacting from a place of confusion or frustration.

THE TEENAGE YEARS

For most people the teenage years mark the beginning of one of the most influential (and painful) periods in determining or realising, our size, weight, shape and eating habits. It is also the time when many of our views about how we see ourselves are formed. And whilst it's healthy to be around our peers, it's unfortunate that at this particular age, those same peers have yet to work out what constitutes friendly banter and what leans towards verbal, emotional and physical abuse. If that weren't enough, every time it seems as though we've got a handle on the way we look, the body changes again, forcing us to reassess the relationship we have with our size and shape. This is not solely a female issue: just as many boys as girls report having these difficulties. The difference is that girls are that much more likely to skip meals and ration their food in an attempt to change the way they look.

Before the age of 11, I'd never thought about my weight. There were a few overweight children at school and I guess my parents had a few overweight friends too, but I'd never really thought about my own weight, shape or size. Then one day, in my first year of secondary school, whilst running down to the games field for a football match, a friend's dad shouted something out to me. It was a comment that stayed with me for years and that I took a long time to let go of. I used to motivate myself with it when I felt I was in good shape, and beat myself up with it when I felt fat. And yet it was just a simple throwaway comment, which I'm quite sure he didn't think about too much before saying, and which he almost certainly didn't think about afterwards. Besides, this was a time when boys were supposed to be strong, impervious to abuse.

As I jogged past him, he looked at me and laughed as he said, 'Blimey, Pudds [my nickname at school], that's a bit of a stomach you've got on you there. You look like a right little porker.' As I looked down at my stomach, I couldn't help thinking he was *right*. The tight nylon polyester football shirt was just stretched over my belly. One little comment, one throwaway remark, which although insensitive, was not meant with any real malice; yet it hurt. It really hurt. And this was despite the fact that I wasn't particularly overweight. It affected my relationship to food in a way he could probably never have imagined. Had I not been surrounded by my peers at the time I would probably have just burst out crying then and there. In that moment I felt weak, insecure, and more than a little unworthy. Most of all, I felt fat. And I didn't like that feeling, not one bit.

Everyone I've spoken to in researching this book has their own story to tell about their teenage years, and I'm quite sure you'll have yours. But no matter what it was, no matter how difficult or how painful it might have been, it's important to acknowledge that it is in the past. That doesn't change the experience, nor does it deny the feelings you may have now in relationship to the experience. What it does do, however, is to allow you to move on. Because so long as you're carrying the baggage of the past around with you, life is going to feel very heavy. Not only that, but the mental commentary that plays the experience over and over again in the mind only reinforces those feelings and the habits that emerged as a result. Mindfulness shows you how to let go of those stories and those feelings and mindful eating will show you what to replace them with instead.

EMOTIONS

This section is arguably worth a chapter of its own. Some of you may even feel it deserves a *book* of its own! Chapter 5 goes into a discussion of emotions in much greater detail, but they are worthy of mention here too.

My guess is that there are very few people living above the poverty line in the developed world who eat out of hunger alone. In fact, I would suggest that most people in this particular demographic eat from a place of emotion. More than that, I would suggest that many of these people choose their food and eat their meals in *direct relationship* to the way they view their size and shape of their body. Now, if the sole motivation of this was out of concern for their wellbeing and the desire to remain fit and healthy, then of course it could be argued that this is a very positive thing. However, if the motivation is driven by strong emotional patterns, feelings of insecurity, low self-esteem, societal pressures and inner conflict, then it's a different matter altogether.

Take a moment to consider again your own motivations for wanting to change the shape of your body. Try not to think of the motivating factors as good or bad, right or wrong. It's as if you just step back for a moment and see them a little more clearly, from an objective point of view. How many of those factors are centred on the health of your heart or the level of your cholesterol? And how many of them are based on the desire to avoid diabetes or hypertension? In contrast, how many of the factors are directly linked to how you see yourself, the shape, size and weight of your body, your level of confidence, the way in which you'd like your friends, family and colleagues to see you, or the type of clothes you'd like to wear? How many of those factors were driven by a subtle (or not so subtle) dislike of yourself? For most people, the cosmetic or aesthetic motivations for dieting will always far outweigh any potential health risks as a motivating factor. The reason for this is simple: they are driven by strong habitual emotions, developed and hardened over the course of a lifetime.

Let's say you're at home alone, and feeling a little blue. What's the first thing you usually do? Most people will look for a way to distract themselves from the feeling. It might be going online, watching some TV, reading a book, or listening to some music. However, those things alone are unlikely to be distracting enough. So what's the next thing you do? If it's heading for the fridge or freezer, without even really being aware of it, then you are not alone. Or what about if you are out and about and you start to feel a little anxious about something? Do you find yourself wandering in to a shop, as if on auto-pilot, determined to find a chocolate bar to take your mind off things? And let's not even go to the stereotypical example of the intense void of loneliness felt at the end of a relationship, which can only be filled by a large tub of sticky toffee, chunky chocolate fudge ice cream.

The truth is, we often do things without being conscious of the thoughts that drive the behaviour. In these situations, we're usually acting out of habit, following well-trodden routes of emotion. They're relatively simple and straightforward tasks that don't require a great deal of focus, and therefore it's relatively easy to do them in a state of 'semi-consciousness'. I'm quite sure that if somebody filmed us acting in this way and replayed it to us, we would be genuinely shocked. We would probably appear like robots, reacting automatically to signals from the brain or cravings from the mind. Just one handful of crisps after the next, one biscuit after the next, one beer after the next, or one chocolate bar after the next.

The problem is that every time we follow a wave of emotion or chain of thought, we are strengthening the habitual pattern. By following it without awareness, we are reaffirming the story in the mind, or the emotional *response* to that story. And this is why mindful eating is so important. It's also why it's so effective. Because it's not about the food you put in your mouth. By that stage the emotion will have built up such a strong sense of momentum that it may well feel almost impossible to withdraw from. Likewise, it's not about trying to convince yourself that you feel differently from the way that you actually feel. Instead, it's about having the awareness to see the formation of the emotion, to see its origins and, with practice, even to see the very first thought that started it all.

Without this awareness we will always miss the initial thought, without this awareness the emotion will always develop and gain momentum, and without this awareness we will always react out of habit. So, being mindful, being aware, allows you to move from a place of knee-jerk reaction, where you are swept away by emotion, to a place of calm, considered response, where you feel confident in holding your ground. It doesn't matter what the emotion is, whether it is one of desire, craving, aversion, guilt, depression, anxiety, anger, boredom or loneliness, the principle is the same, and the processes at play are no different from one to the next.

LACK OF EXERCISE

We live in a world that encourages us to do *less* exercise, that pushes us to be *more* sedentary, and that consistently delivers products, gadgets and contraptions enabling us to be *less* active. Sure, there's the voice of the fitness industry, the advice of government, the medical profession and other health agencies, even of popular books and magazines. But these voices are often drowned out by the noise that urges us to *do less and eat more*.

In my late teens I spent a lot of time living in America. I still remember the first time I went to the shopping mall. I would see people come out of one shop, get in their car, drive maybe 20 or 30 metres further along in the car park, and then walk in to the next shop. I could hardly believe what I was seeing. Everybody drove, no matter how short the distance, and no matter how urgent the need for physical exercise. In one town where I lived, there wasn't even a pavement. After a few weeks of stubbornly walking in the roadside and several near misses with oncoming traffic unfamiliar with the sight of pedestrians in the road, I eventually relented and got in a car.

If society does not encourage us to be active, to get physical, then that is just one more obstacle to us achieving optimum health. And this is a pattern that is repeated throughout every demographic in society. Many children no longer play freely and actively with their friends. Whether that's to do with concerns over safety, the increasingly popularity of computer games or the urbanisation of many rural areas, it's hard to say. But one thing is for sure: the increased reliance on and use of computers and handheld electronic devices are changing the physiology of the next generation. Bodies that were designed and programmed to be physical and active are now learning new ways of sedentary behaviour that will inevitably impact the health of those individuals. It will have an impact in the short term, as the obesity statistics for children clearly demonstrate, but it will also have a long-term effect, creating habitual patterns of behaviour for the next generation that will potentially last a lifetime.

But what about *this* generation? Is it already too late? We know what we need to do, what we 'should' be doing in order to be more healthy, but how often does it actually happen? The busiest time for health clubs is usually around January, the time of New Year resolutions, when most people seem to have a great enthusiasm for losing weight. But how long do those efforts usually last? The rates of attrition at the gym are not unlike those of popular diets. In fact I once heard a gym manager joke that it was not the people that came to the gym on a regular basis that enabled them to make a profit, but rather the countless millions who sign up for gym membership and then never show up.

In many ways it's tragic that we should even need to go and create such a contrived form of exercise in an artificial environment like a gym. But the reality of modern-day living suggests that it is one of the few ways we can achieve the volume of exercise necessary to maintain optimum health and fitness.

Needless to say, if you can think of something else, a sport or activity away from the gym that you enjoy and can be actively engaged in on a regular basis, then all the better – even if that's just going for a good brisk walk each day. And, contrary to popular opinion, it really is quite OK to *enjoy* physical exercise! Unfortunately, there is now such a strong feeling of obligation for many people, that exercise has lost a lot of its fun. Added to that, many people resent being told what to do, lack the self-confidence to go in to that environment, or perhaps still have recurring nightmares about physical education at school. But once all that stuff has been let go of, exercise will prove to be one of your very best supports in achieving your ideal weight, size and shape.

ADDICTIONS

Addiction is a word that needs to be used sparingly, as with labels of any kind, especially the negative variety, as they simply reinforce the belief that the behaviour is part of who you are (as opposed to a temporary habitual state, capable of change). However, there is no question that some people follow an addictive pattern of behaviour with certain foods, or feel so overwhelmed by the desire to eat that they feel powerless to prevent themselves from doing so.

It can be the intense craving for the next hit of sugar (often in the form of a chocolate bar or fizzy drink), the need to feel the rush of caffeine in your bloodstream, the irresistible urge to add salt to your plate, or the desire to consume a food that you associate closely with a particular emotion (otherwise known as comfort eating). Whatever the driving force for picking up the spoon, opening up the packet, or lifting the cup, the sensation is one of desperation, and the feeling is one of inevitability.

There are several factors at work in this process and it's useful to separate them out. One of them relates very specifically to the dynamics of both body and mind, something covered in more detail in Chapters 5 and 6, but for now I'd just like to focus on the external factors involved, that of the big business food industry. I'm not talking about all the wonderful ethical initiatives that are taking place around the world which are encouraging us to change the way we shop, cook, eat and relate to our food. Neither am I suggesting that there is some kind of global conspiracy amongst big business to further addiction and to encourage us to eat more unhealthy foods.

The food industry exists to sell food. Like any other 'for-profit' business, they work to sell more units of their products, to develop foods that are irresistible, to encourage us to buy them, so that they can then make more money. It's a very simple equation. However, unlike most businesses they have the unique advantage of selling us something that we *need* to stay alive. So, it should come as no great surprise that the products on offer have been developed to taste and appear as attractive and appetising as possible. After all, the food industry doesn't just want us to buy *one* of these products, it wants us to buy *lots* of these products. And if it can persuade us to buy so many products that we begin to feel overweight, then it always has the option of selling us one of its low-fat varieties, or weight-loss options. Cynical? Perhaps. Factual? I think it's hard to argue with any one of those statements.

With this in mind, please don't beat yourself up for feeling 'addicted' to certain foods. They are *designed* to create that response. This is precision engineering: perfectly balanced quantities of fat, sugar, salt and additives, mixed together in such a way that it makes them appear quite irresistible. By recognising and acknowledging this simple fact, you are immediately released from any feelings of weakness, inadequacy or failure. After all, how could you not keep going back for more? Making you go back for more is exactly what the product is designed to do. Fortunately, mindfulness allows us to break this cycle.

ALCOHOL

There is a certain subsection of the food industry that relies on people drinking alcohol. It mostly consists of the fast-food outlets, burger vans and doner-kebab shops located right next door to busy pubs and clubs. These are often places that we wouldn't touch with a bargepole during the day and yet, after a few drinks, it suddenly seems like such a good idea. Alcohol not only weakens our sense of will, purpose and direction, but it also makes it more difficult to be aware of our mind states. It creates a mind that is open to suggestion, more willing to throw caution to the wind. In short, alcohol is responsible for a lot of very bad choices. That doesn't mean you shouldn't enjoy a drink or two once in a while, but it does mean that if you are serious about being more mindful around food, then moderating your alcohol consumption is a must.

Perhaps the days of going out drinking are already long behind you and now it's more likely to be a couple of glasses of wine whilst relaxing on the sofa in the evening. But take a moment to think what normally accompanies that drink. Is it a bowl of crisps or nuts? A takeaway, perhaps? Unhealthy food choices and alcohol seem to go hand-in-hand. When was the last time you sat down and enjoyed carrot and celery sticks (without any dip) whilst drinking a glass of wine or pint of beer? Exactly. Again, I'm not saying that it's a bad thing, that we shouldn't do it, but we need to be aware that these alcohol-induced food choices will inevitably influence the way we look and feel about ourselves.

But the way in which alcohol *really* has the potential to derail any attempts to change your shape or weight lies in the so-called hidden calories. It's hard to find a more concentrated source of calories than alcohol. Not only that, but a concentrated source that has so little nutritional value. In just one night those excess calories are likely to make little difference to your size and shape, but when consumed on a regular basis, it cannot help but change the way you look.

If calm and clarity is what we're looking for, if stability of emotion is what we crave, and if we are in any way serious about developing a healthy relationship with both food and our body, then necking copious amounts of alcohol on a regular basis is never going to help.

SOCIAL PRESSURE

It doesn't matter whether it's a business meeting, a weekend catch-up with friends, a birthday celebration with family, video night with your partner, or a rendezvous with a lover, the way we eat with others has a significant impact on our weight, shape and size. We make choices that we would never make if we were eating alone and we eat with only a fraction of the awareness that we might do so usually. Food is such an incredibly social thing. Whether meeting in an office, at home, in a coffee shop, a restaurant, or a park, there's pretty much always some kind of food around – even if it's only a biscuit with a cup of tea. In many ways this is a very comforting thing, something that we all share together.

However, left unchecked it can easily scupper any plans you have to reach your ideal size. Part of this can be a feeling that the other person (or people) somehow give us *permission* to eat the foods we wouldn't normally eat on our own. There's a feeling of, 'Well, if *they're* going for the deep-fried Mars bar with ice cream, then so am I.' At other times it can be a feeling of obligation, to keep the other person company or to keep things flowing smoothly in a meeting. More often than not, though, it is simply a loss of awareness as the excitement or intensity of conversation takes over and we just reach out for handful after handful of nuts or crisps.

Sharing food is a wonderful, precious thing, and I am not discouraging it in any way. Nor am I discouraging a sense of relaxation and freedom when you meet and eat with others. What I *am* saying, however, is that it is often in these situations that we lose our way with food and make choices that we later regret. Being aware of this can help us approach those times with a greater sense of calm, clear about what choices are going to best reflect our underlying values and wishes. And, if we still decide to go for that second dessert – well, at least we'll be doing it consciously, and fully aware of the consequences.

LAZINESS

Now you might just be the most productive, efficient and focused person you know. You might also have bundles of energy and an unbridled enthusiasm for life. But even with all those qualities, you may still find yourself, every now and then, thinking: 'You know, I just can't be bothered to cook tonight.' It doesn't make you a bad person, or even a lazy person. In fact it actually makes you a refreshingly normal person. That said, fleeting moments of laziness or indifference around this one particular aspect of life is one of the biggest contributors to weight gain, and it's important to see it for what it really is.

We've all been there: it's been a long day, you've been on your feet for hours on end, and all you want to do is sit down and eat. You don't want to have to think about shopping for food, preparing food, or cooking food. On these days, even opening the microwave door and pushing a few buttons can seem like hard work. This isn't such a big problem, and it's a perfectly natural feeling after all. But it's how we *relate* to the feeling that can cause the difficulty. Because if we react to the feeling with a knee-jerk 'don't mind, don't care, whatever' attitude, then our food choices will reflect this sentiment. And when it comes to your body, you almost certainly *do* mind, *do* care and would rarely settle for *whatever*.

This is where mindfulness comes into its own again. If you can *see* the feeling of laziness or indifference, as opposed to identifying so strongly with the feeling that you *become* lazy or indifferent, then you have the opportunity to respond with a sense of calm. That may well mean that you still choose to go for a quick and easy microwave meal, and that's fine. The difference will be that, rather than grabbing a pizza or a burger, you are that much more likely to make a healthy choice that directly reflects your underlying motivation and goals, than if you simply followed the usual habitual patterns.

SLEEP

You may well be wondering how sleep can impact on weight and eating habits. It might be tempting to assume that I'm talking about too *much* sleep, and therefore not enough exercise and a slow metabolism. But actually, it turns out to be the reverse. Researchers have recently discovered that it's when people are sleeping *less*, for shorter periods of time, not long enough for the body to fully recover and recuperate, that the accumulation of body fat appears to increase – and by up to 32 per cent.

These scientists also found that by having a full night of restful sleep, the effects of any inherited 'obesity genes' can actually be offset. Although they are still not entirely sure why this is or how it happens, what they *do* know is that when we are in sleep deficit, we metabolise more muscle and less fat. According to one particular study, in less than two weeks of having their sleep disturbed on a nightly basis, participants increased their weight by an average of three pounds.

But there's a secondary impact of sleep that is equally important. Because research has also shown that when people suffer from a lot of daytime sleepiness, they are far more likely to crave high-sugar foodstuffs. The consequence is that they then become locked into a cycle of eating, where they alternate between sugar highs and sugar lows. Ultimately, this leads to a less healthy diet, a greater consumption of calorie-dense foods, and an increase in weight and size. It also creates a very 'reactive' behavioural pattern towards food and eating habits, which makes it that much more difficult to respond with calm and clarity. In turn, this makes it harder to make the positive choices that will enable you to look the way you'd like to look, and to feel the way you'd like to feel. But then that's the great thing about mindful eating – not only will it help you to get in shape, it may just help you sleep better too.

STRESS

When are you most likely to make food choices that you will later regret? When do you tend to indulge in negative eating patterns that you wish you could change? When are you most likely to put off physical exercise because you don't feel like it or haven't got time? If you're like most people, it won't be when you're feeling good about yourself and pleased with how you're coping with life. It will be when you feel stressed, overworked and under pressure. It will be in those moments when there is very little *calm*, when your thoughts have caused a feeling of agitation or restlessness on the surface of the mind. Likewise, it will be in those moments when there is very little *clarity*, when the mind is in a typically 'reactive' state, as opposed to a considered 'responsive' state. So it should come as no surprise that weight gain is not only a *cause* of great stress, but is also a *symptom* of great stress.

The stress response is familiar to most of us and, if you

regularly find yourself getting a little uptight, then you're in good company. A large survey carried out by the UK Mental Health Foundation in 2010 found that well over 80 per cent of people felt as though the speed of life and overwhelming number of commitments was a major cause of stress, unhappiness and illness. More than half of the people in the survey said that they simply didn't know how to switch off and relax. Again, that's where the real value of mindfulness comes into play, but more of that later. In the meantime, what are the implications of this for our diet, how does stress influence our eating choices and what does stress do to the body that makes it so difficult to lose weight?

In the short term, stress causes the delicate balance of hormones and chemicals in the body to be thrown out of line. One of the most important chemical reactions taking place at a time of stress is the release of cortisol, often known as the 'stress hormone'. Although we need cortisol to live, when it's produced in excess quantities or over a sustained period of time, then it begins to have a really detrimental effect on the body. It interferes with the digestion of food, sometimes halting it altogether. It can also lead to food cravings and has been shown in multiple scientific studies to be a significant factor in people putting on weight. In fact it creates the worst possible conditions for weight loss or weight maintenance. Because it actually speeds up and encourages the accumulation of fat around the waistline, whilst at the same time playing an instrumental role in breaking down your highly prized lean muscle. This is the exact opposite of what you will no doubt be trying to achieve.

As for the long-term effects of stress, you'll probably already know that it has been found to increase blood pressure, elevate cholesterol levels, as well as increase the incidence of strokes and coronary heart disease. It has also been shown to adversely impact the immune system, leaving us more vulnerable to infection. More recently, stress has been shown to reduce the chances of couples conceiving. It's usually at this point that someone will say, 'But isn't stress a good thing sometimes?' Well, only you know how it feels to be stressed, and whether you consider that to be healthy or pleasant. Is it good to feel challenged, motivated, focused, with a sense of purpose in life? Of course it is, and if that's what you mean by stress then, in the right quantities, it is a good thing. But if we are talking about feeling overwhelmed, unhappy, tense, tired or exhausted, then I don't think you'll find many people who view stress as something positive.

In sharp contrast to the short-term chemical reactions of the 'stress response', the technique and practice of mindfulness has been shown to invoke something called the 'relaxation response'. This tends to cause a series of physical reactions that most of us would associate with a greater feeling of comfort and ease. For example, high blood pressure tends to decrease, breathing begins to slow down, muscle tension is released and the body goes into a positive cycle of wellbeing. This means that the mind recognises that the body is relaxing and therefore relaxes itself, which in turn reinforces and further promotes relaxation in the body. And so it continues in a very positive loop, with body and mind winding down and easing up. It is in this state that the body is able to maintain lean muscle mass, whilst more easily losing body fat.

CHAPTER FOUR

THE HEADSPACE FOOD TEST: HOW DO YOU EAT YOURS?

If the last chapter was all about identifying the many factors that have influenced the way in which you eat, this chapter is all about identifying how that unique combination of factors has left you feeling, and what tendencies it has led to.

So, what kind of eater are you? What attitude do you have towards your body? And what attitude do you have towards dieting? Each of us has a unique mix of the factors outlined in the previous chapter, making us more likely to reach for a slice of pizza rather than some vegetables, or for some ice cream instead of an apple. Likewise, whilst some will happily gorge for days, others will abstain to the point of dizziness and hunger pangs. And whilst some people *live* for food, savouring every last mouthful and always thinking of what to try next, others do everything they can to avoid food, searching for excuses not to eat. Some people even use nicotine and caffeine in an attempt to curb eating, whilst others spend their lives pounding the pavements or pumping iron in order that they can then eat more having burnt extra calories. For each and every person, there's a different approach to food. So what type of foodie are you?

This is not about finding a label that you can proudly wear, identifying yourself as a certain kind of *person*. It is more to do with recognising and acknowledging certain *tendencies* you may already have, that will then help you to make the changes you want to make. Read through the following descriptions and start to notice which types feel most appropriate to you and your current eating habits. You may find that you don't fit neatly in to any one of the categories listed here. In fact, you might find that there are certain aspects of *many* which best suit your character, eating habits, and attitudes towards dieting. That's absolutely fine; this chapter is not designed to squeeze you into a box or a category, but rather to get you thinking about *how* you eat, *what* you eat and *why* you eat. Likewise, to acknowledge your attitude to dieting and the relative merits or disadvantages of such an approach. You might like to flick back to it every now and then, as you embark and continue with the 10-Day Plan.

A Note on Scoring:

All of the different Foodie Types in this chapter have been given both a Headspace Mindfulness Score and a Headspace Health Score. These scores reflect the likely level of mindfulness of that particular character type, and the potential health impact of living that way. The scores are measured on a scale of 1 to 10, with 1 being the worst possible score, and 10 being the best possible score.

THE NIBBLER

Characteristics

Sometimes known as the Grazer, the Nibbler is always eating *something*. Avoiding large meals, through fear of consuming too much and putting on weight, they instead choose to snack throughout the entire day. Nibblers are usually the ones carrying nuts, seeds and carrot sticks with them, but there are also those who graze on less wholesome snacks.

Typical Inner Dialogue

'Now where did I put those spelt crackers? Maybe I should give myself a little pick-me-up and have some chocolate instead . . . I'll just have a little bit to keep me going, just to keep my blood-sugar levels up. Could do with a bit more energy, but don't want to feel bloated again – maybe a few pumpkin seeds would be better . . . '

Advantages

Constant stimulation of the metabolism can increase your base metabolic rate – at least in theory. Also great for those with a busy schedule and no time to stop and eat a meal. In the past there was a lot of discussion as to whether this was a healthier and more natural way of eating, but as yet there is no strong scientific evidence to suggest this is the case.

Disadvantages

Often consuming more calories than the same person following a more traditional eating plan, the Nibbler is at risk of overstimulating desire. Always eating, or thinking about eating, reinforces neural pathways and encourages that behaviour. Due to an over-reliance on snack foods, Nibblers will sometimes need to resort to unhealthy food choices.

Attitude to Dieting

The Nibbler will often reject more formal and structured diet plans, assuming that their own technique of grazing is better. However, as grazing like this rarely works in the way intended, it usually leads to a feeling of failure or disappointment when it comes to weight loss. For most Nibblers, this style of eating is nothing short of a way of life.

Day-to-Day Awareness

Nibblers are usually very aware of body shape, size and weight, but out of tune with natural feelings of hunger and satisfaction. They are not always good at listening to the body and will snack on foods without being fully aware of whether they're hungry or not. The mind is often in a state of desire or restless agitation, looking for, or thinking of, the next thing to eat.

Headspace Mindfulness Score: 3
Headspace Health Score: 5

THE GORGER

Characteristics

Like a Nibbler on steroids, the Gorger is always eating, but by no means grazing. Although often desperate to lose weight, they tend to eat in a self-destructive way, consuming large volumes of calorie-dense, highly processed foods – often of the fast-food variety. The Gorger is typically aware of this situation, but too overwhelmed to change their behaviour.

Typical Inner Dialogue

'Wow, I could murder a double cheeseburger with extra onions and relish right now . . . maybe some fries . . . some fried bacon – I'm starting to salivate just thinking about it. I wish I wasn't so fat . . . I guess I could always go to the Weight Watchers' meeting later and confess. Oooo, and maybe I'll get a milkshake with that burger too.'

Advantages

Clearly, there are no advantages whatsoever to eating in this way.

Disadvantages

Eating calorie-rich, highly processed foods in such large quantities will inevitably lead to health risks, ranging from obesity, to high blood pressure and heart disease. This type of eating is likely to be driven by habitual patterns of thought and strong emotional triggers.

Typically, it will perpetuate feelings of self-loathing and low self-esteem.

Attitude to Dieting

The Gorger is not immune to dieting and will, on occasion, follow a restrictive diet of some kind. This usually lasts for only a *very* short period of time and has little or no useful impact on their long-term eating habits. Almost inevitably overweight, the Gorger usually wants to eat less, but the overwhelming strength of emotion can make it feel impossible.

Day-to-Day Awareness

Some call it denial, while others call it indulgence. Whichever it is, the Gorger is not living life in the present. With strong addictive/compulsive tendencies, they tend to be swept away by feelings of desire, leading to self-destructive behaviour, which can be a cause of great unhappiness, confusion and mental unrest.

Headspace Mindfulness Score: 2
Headspace Health Score: 1

THE DIET JUNKIE

Characteristics

The Diet Junkie, not to be confused with the Calorie Counter can be identified by the latest diet sensation or populist weight-loss book they are holding. As the name suggests, they are *addicted* to dieting, convinced that the next programme will be *the one*! Unconcerned with sustenance and nutritional content, the Diet Junkie views food (or the lack of it) purely as a vehicle to weight loss.

Typical Inner Dialogue

'As soon as I finish this giant multipack, I am going *straight* on that new diet. If they're doing it in Hollywood, then it's good enough for me. Bring on the red carpet, baby! I can't believe what's-her-name dropped four dress sizes on it. That's insane. Oh my god, I'm going to look so thin. Maybe what's-his-face will finally realise what he's missing . . . '

Advantages
Put simply, there really are no advantages to be found in following one dieting regime after the next, other than for the sheer novelty value.

Disadvantages
The Diet Junkie is likely to suffer from a lack of sustenance, nutritional variety and consistency. As a result, the body will often be in 'protective mode', holding on to every last ounce of fat. Emotionally, feelings of dissatisfaction, disappointment, anxiety and guilt come as standard for a Diet Junkie, and feelings of having failed repeatedly can erode self-esteem over time.

Attitude to Dieting
Excellent at following prescribed diet plans for short periods of time, Diet Junkies will eat anything, everything or nothing, in a bid to lose weight. Quickly bored and dissatisfied, they are likely to 'diet-hop' from one plan to the next. They will typically follow a yo-yo diet mentality, making the maintenance of any weight loss almost impossible.

Day-to-Day Awareness
Forget the here and now, the Diet Junkie lives only for the future. Permanently looking forward to the next miracle weight-loss cure and the illusive dream of perfection, their happiness is

often directly related to their weight, size and shape. A lack of awareness can prove to be both a source, and a cause, of considerable unhappiness for the Diet Junkie.

Headspace Mindfulness Score: 2
Headspace Health Score: 2

THE ECO-GEEK

Characteristics
Currently in the ascendancy, the Eco-Geek is a model of mindful shopping, ethical values and sustainable consumerism. They are frequently (but not necessarily) vegetarian, or even vegan, and would not be seen anywhere near the high-street supermarkets. Highly unlikely to be overweight, they tend to eat a diet that is well balanced and rich in nutrients.

Typical Inner Dialogue
'Better sort my stuff out for yoga – my downward dog is really coming on. Damn, gotta stop thinking of yoga in that way – learn to just "be". That reminds me, I must buy some of that Manuka honey – supposed to be packed full of antioxidants and I bet it'll be amazing on those organic, Fairtrade, gluten-free, dairy-free spelt crackers. Can't wait!'

Advantages
A diet that is rich in natural foods and diversity has many advantages for both the body and mind. An Eco-Geek will have no trouble maintaining a healthy weight and will benefit from

stable blood-sugar levels. Just as importantly, though, this approach also fosters a wider perspective that takes into account the impact our eating has on the planet.

Disadvantages
Nutritional deficiencies can arise from time to time with this type of eating and it is not uncommon to require more protein, as well as higher levels of minerals such as iron. Unfortunately, the Eco-Geek approach can sometimes encourage a slightly militant and judgemental attitude towards other types of foodies.

Attitude to Dieting
The Eco-Geek is very unlikely to participate in any form of dieting, but may well be tempted by the idea of fasting. Just as keen to stay in shape as the next person (but claiming otherwise), they are likely to exercise regularly and choose foods that not only benefit the planet, but also benefit their waistlines.

Day-to-Day Awareness
With a keen awareness of the outer world as well as the inner, the Eco-Geek scores very highly in this department. They are likely to make food choices from a place of well-considered thought and will be sensitive to their levels of hunger and satiety. Any mental chatter about food and the body will be about more than just weight loss alone.

Headspace Mindfulness Score: 7
Headspace Health Score: 8

THE GYM BUNNY

Characteristics

The Gym Bunny exercises regularly and moderately, but their relationship with food is still dictated by their training and their body image. Food choices tend to be well considered and chosen with body shape in mind.

Typical Inner Dialogue

'Wow, these chocolate biscuits are amazing! OK, now it looks as though each one is about 30 calories – wow, that's more than I thought – so that's an extra 10 minutes per biscuit on the treadmill, so if I get out of here at 5.30, then I can squeeze in an extra 30 minutes at the gym. That's three whole biscuits . . . totally worth it, though.'

Advantages

Eating a wide range of unrefined foods, and usually plenty of fruits and vegetables too, the Gym Bunny usually eats a well-proportioned diet, incorporating all the major food groups. They also tend to have positive lifestyle values and experience relatively good emotional health.

Disadvantages

A Gym Bunny typically weighs up the value of a food by calculating the number of minutes it will take to run it off in the gym. This mind-set of justification leaves little room for appreciation. Because of the strong desire to reach a certain shape, they are typically caught in a cycle of hope and fear – hopeful that they'll make it, fearful that they won't.

Attitude to Dieting

The Gym Bunny is rarely overweight and unlikely to be an early adopter of fad diets. That said, most female Gym Bunnies wouldn't be averse to incorporating some of the elements if they thought it might make a difference, whereas male Gym Bunnies tend to be less flexible. Any dieting by either sex is likely to be motivated by aesthetics.

Day-to-Day Awareness

Although their motivation for eating may well be questionable, their awareness of food, nutrition, eating patterns and body image is undoubtedly high. However, due to the 'food = fuel' mentality, they will often lack awareness in the process of eating itself and will therefore be unaccustomed to eating mindfully.

Headspace Mindfulness Score: 6
Headspace Health Score: 8

THE BINGER

Characteristics

Surprisingly, the Binger often eats a very *healthy* diet (when they're not binging, that is). In fact, they will generally follow very strict diet regimens, which require a great deal of willpower, punctuated by bouts of the opposing behaviour. It is a life of extremes, swinging from excessive control to a feeling of powerlessness.

Typical Inner Dialogue

'Wow, this new diet has been amazing! I'm so much thinner! I think I probably deserve a chocolate, just to say well done. Mmmmm, I'd forgotten how good these taste . . . hello my old friend . . . maybe just one more, and one more . . . and one last one – might as well finish the box . . . need more chocolate. Maybe I can scrape the chocolate off these biscuits . . .'

Advantages

Most of the time, the Binger will manage their eating very well and consume foods with a high nutritional content, from all the major food groups. In fact, this can often represent up to 90 per cent of their eating habits. This means that meals will be taken regularly, be balanced in terms of diversity and will usually omit most processed and refined foodstuffs.

Disadvantages

Sadly, even the healthiest of diets can be utterly derailed by a few moments of madness every now and then. This is a style of eating that comes loaded with emotional baggage, often including strong feelings of guilt and shame, together with excessive mind chatter. The high-sugar binge foods are also likely to have an addictive effect on the body.

Attitude to Dieting

The Binger loves to diet. In a world where they often feel out of control, a strict course of prescribed eating brings the sense of order and structure that they desperately seek in themselves. However, diets typically end in binges, reinforcing that sense of failure that will ultimately perpetuate and encourage more of the same binging mentality.

Day-to-Day Awareness

Often acutely aware of their destructive eating patterns, the Binger will generally be very vigilant in their approach to food. Throughout the non-binging phases, they will typically enjoy a healthy perspective on their behaviour. However, this perspective lacks stability and can unravel at a moment's notice. This is the importance of being mindful throughout the day.

Headspace Mindfulness Score: 5
Headspace Health Score: 4

THE SOCIALITE

Characteristics

Socialites don't really *do* food. Sure, they might nibble on a few canapés between glasses of wine at a party, but they generally view food as the work of the devil. Perhaps overly concerned with how they look (to both themselves and others), the Socialite's food plan is based on cosmetic weight loss and aesthetics. Cigarettes often replace eating.

Typical Inner Dialogue

'Really can't be bothered to cook tonight. I wonder if what's-her-chops is coming to the pub – maybe we can nip out and get some frozen yoghurt or something later, or maybe I'll just have another vodka instead . . . Wow, my liver must be properly fried: killer ass, though, and have got to get into that dress for Friday. That reminds me, where's my trainer's number?'

Advantages

This is a diet that requires very little organisation, preparation, cooking – or even eating for that matter. For the busy networker, highly pressured business person, or social addict, this can at first appear an attractive option.

Disadvantages

The Socialite's diet is likely to be deficient in just about everything other than alcohol and nicotine. Typically skipping both breakfast and lunch, they will often snack on unhealthy foods. As a result, blood-sugar levels are likely to be extremely unstable, leading to mood swings and occasionally insomnia. High levels of anxiety are commonplace.

Attitude to Dieting

The Socialite is more likely to be underweight than overweight. However, a slim waist should not be confused with low body fat and, proportionately, they are every bit as likely to suffer from excess body fat. Quickly bored and easily dissatisfied, dieting presents many challenges for the Socialite; however, they will want to be the first to try out anything new.

Day-to-Day Awareness

The Socialite is acutely aware of their size and shape, but is ironically too caught up in thinking about these things to be aware of the behaviours that could actually affect it. Often coming from a place of low self-esteem, insecurity or competitiveness, the Socialite will usually be very strong-willed and highly controlling in nature.

Headspace Mindfulness Score: 4
Headspace Health Score: 2

THE ZOMBIE

Characteristics
Just as the name suggests, Zombies are barely conscious of what foods they consume. It is as if the body and mind are on autopilot: everything is done out of habit or routine. Zombies tend to have a very monotonous diet, lacking many of the important nutrients; their eating is devoid of any real pleasure or appreciation. In short, it is eating for the sake of eating.

Typical Inner Dialogue
'Wow, long day today, wonder what's on telly tonight . . . she looks nice . . . it's really warm this evening. Wish this queue wasn't so long . . . hey, where did she go? Every day the same old bus ride . . . thank goodness for these new apps, Hang on a minute, I don't remember buying deep-fried cheese sticks, chunky-wedge chips, mayonnaise and ice cream! Oh well . . . '

Advantages
This way of eating requires very little thought, planning or organisation. There is also rarely any preparation or cooking

involved (the use of the microwave being a notable exception). This means that Zombies are time-rich when it comes to eating, even if they are lacking the necessary nutrients to live healthily.

Disadvantages

For anyone wanting to lose weight, this approach to food is a recipe for disaster. The Zombie is often unaware of thoughts and feelings about eating, and is rarely fully conscious when buying or consuming food, which hampers genuine change. Zombies also tend to eat highly processed, refined foods, which lack nutritional value.

Attitude to Dieting

Zombies have no interest in nutrition, but are nonetheless conscious of body shape. They are highly unlikely to engage in diets of any kind and are often overweight. It is common for Zombies to experience low self-esteem and unhappiness, and also to harbour underlying anxieties in relation to the way they look during fleeting moments of awareness.

Day-to-Day Awareness

Whether it is through ignoring the reality of weight gain, being immersed in something else so completely that food and diet become unimportant, or following an emotional pattern of indifference, the Zombie is rarely in the here and now. This leads to poor food choices, bad eating habits, and often ill-health.

Headspace Mindfulness Score: 1
Headspace Health Score: 1

THE CALORIE COUNTER

Characteristics

The Calorie Counter is obsessive in nature, and able to tell you, to the nearest nanogram, the ingredients of any given food. In fact, they will examine the underside of food packaging with a microscope, conscious not only of the calorie count, but also the nutritional content. Their natural habitat is the low-fat aisle of the supermarket or the local health-food store.

Typical Inner Dialogue

'Wish I hadn't eaten that extra-low-fat, sample-size portion of pudding last night. Guess I should take it a bit easy at lunch today and have just the one stick of celery with my cottage cheese. That'll be 150 calories, plus 45 for the celery, plus the pudding from last night, but minus the roast potatoes I managed to avoid over at mum's the other day . . .'

Advantages

In many ways, the diet of a Calorie Counter is extremely healthy, with well-balanced meals at regular intervals, consisting of highly nutritious foods. By necessity, they tend to plan far ahead and are therefore organised in their preparation of food. This style of eating tends to ensure that they maintain stable blood-sugar levels and so rarely feel hungry.

Disadvantages

For all that is good in their diet, such a fanatical approach to food suggests a relationship that is somewhat out of balance.

The Calorie Counter will devote a disproportionate amount of time and headspace to food and weight loss and is particularly prone to anxiety. Such a rigid and inflexible approach typically leads to a great deal of internal conflict.

Attitude to Dieting

The life of a Calorie Counter is one long diet, so they are usually immune to more faddish diets. Extremely attached to this way of eating, it is usually reflected in other lifestyle choices too. For example, they are highly unlikely to smoke, even less likely to drink, and will usually exercise regularly. These are seen as essential aids to the ultimate goal in life.

Day-to-Day Awareness

Whilst you might expect the level of awareness to be high, such strong, obsessive thoughts often clouds awareness, making it impossible to see things clearly. And, unsurprisingly, a relationship with so many rules and expectations is rarely a happy one. The Calorie Counter is likely to have a strong compulsive nature, and not just towards food.

Headspace Mindfulness Score: 5
Headspace Health Score: 7

THE GOURMET

Characteristics

They know what they like, and they know how to get it. The Gourmet will eat only the best, even if it means taking out an overdraft to pay for it. A great deal of time is spent thinking about food, talking about food, and eating food, with little or no consideration as to where the food has come from or the effect it will have on the body. Such is the life of the Gourmet.

Typical Inner Dialogue

'Think I'll head over to that nice Italian tonight, or maybe I'll do sushi instead. I wonder if they've got that special fish on at the moment. The guy on that wildlife programme the other day said it was almost extinct – better not die out before I get some! That reminds me, I should pick up some veal on the way home . . . '

Advantages

The Gourmet has the dubious luxury of eating expensive, unusual, and hard-to-source foods. This allows for an extensive knowledge and understanding of different cuisines in terms of tastes, although rarely in terms of nutritional content and after-effects. It tends to be a varied diet which, as long as the right types of foods are eaten, has the potential to be beneficial.

Disadvantages

Largely unconcerned with the nutrients they consume, and regularly eating out, the Gourmet tends to eat a heavy diet, rich in fat and sugar. Whilst it may not be the highly processed variety, it is nonetheless difficult for the body to process and can rapidly lead to weight gain. There are also the broader social and ethical questions to consider.

Attitude to Dieting

The Gourmet views the concept of dieting as laughable. They will tell you that life is too short, that food is to be enjoyed, and that you don't need to worry about the future (even if that future *does* involve you needing foie gras-inspired heart surgery). It's all about priorities, and for a Gourmet, food tops weight loss every time.

Day-to-Day Awareness

With a keen sense of awareness whilst eating, the Gourmet will tend to be highly attuned to the smells, flavours and tastes of food. However, unfortunately their enthusiasm often spills over from appreciation to indulgence. And let's not forget the excessive and habitual thinking about food, which fills every waking moment.

Headspace Mindfulness Score: 5
Headspace Health Score: 4

THE BEAR

Characteristics

Much like its hibernating namesake, the Bear just can't seem to get the metabolic engine running. Whilst there are those who eat constantly and still lose weight, the Bear can eat surprisingly little and yet still pile on the pounds. Because of this they tend to eat a very restricted diet, which often belies their shape and size.

Typical Inner Dialogue

'It's just not fair. I've hardly eaten anything for weeks now and my weight's just not budging. How can that skinny little thing in the office get away with stuffing her face with cream buns, whilst all I eat is yoghurt and fruit and I look like this? Seriously, there's just no justice in this world. I might just as well stuff my face with cream buns . . . '

Advantages

Other than being very aware of the foods they consume, it is difficult to find any real advantages of eating so sparingly, regardless of shape, weight, size or body image.

Disadvantages

When the body is continually deprived of calories, it essentially powers down. This means the metabolism is reduced so as not to use up its precious reserves of energy. Good news for the survival of our species, bad news for weight loss. And then there's all that emotional baggage. Feelings of failure, frustration, depression and guilt are all common.

Attitude to Dieting

The Bear is very self-conscious. Despite being cynical of dieting, they will nonetheless try anything new, searching for that 'miracle cure'. Physical exercise would be the best way of kick-starting the metabolism, but very few Bears have the confidence to engage in physical activity. The focus needs to shift from 'calories consumed' to 'hours active'.

Day-to-Day Awareness

Whilst acutely aware of the food they consume, Bears are rarely aware of their self-perpetuating habits and will struggle to let go of them. They are usually hyper-aware of their body shape, but will distort the reality by projecting images in the mind that reflect their frustrations with the slow pace of weight loss. There is usually little calm and clarity.

Headspace Mindfulness Score: 4
Headspace Health Score: 3

THE COMFORT EATER

Characteristics

Rarely eating from a place of hunger, the Comfort Eater consumes food from a place of emotion. Looking to fill some kind of void, or to distract themselves from acknowledging painful and difficult feelings, they eat as a form of emotional management. It is rarely a healthy diet, consisting mostly of highly refined and overly processed foods.

Typical Inner Dialogue

'I'm bored . . . where are the biscuits? I can't believe he said that to me earlier . . . where are the crisps? And how am I supposed to stay on top of all this work . . . where are those muffins? God, I wish I had somebody to talk to about all this . . . maybe some cheese will cheer me up. I really shouldn't be eating all this stuff; I feel so guilty . . . '

Advantages

Other than the (very) temporary and (very) fleeting relief from a particularly troubling emotion, there is no advantage to eating in this way at all.

Disadvantages

The Comfort Eater will often deny themselves good, healthy, balanced meals, at the expense of a continuous stream of snacks and highly processed foods. Lacking in nutrition, it is often a diet high in calories. Simply avoiding or displacing an emotion does not get rid of it. At best it keeps it at bay, but at worst it actually strengthens it.

Attitude to Dieting

Most Comfort Eaters will jump at the chance of trying out a new diet, but attempts are typically short-lived. Largely out of touch with the usual hunger signals of the body, and feeling powerless in the face of emotion, they will usually find it very difficult to stick to any prescribed plan of eating. Ironically, they will then comfort eat in an attempt to feel better.

Day-to-Day Awareness

Emotion can never be processed through the consumption of food, no matter how tasty it might be. In fact the Comfort Eater is rarely even aware of this tendency to eat from a place of emotion. Pushing with one hand and pulling with the other (both literally and metaphorically), the mind-set is usually one of discursiveness and confusion.

Headspace Mindfulness Score: 2
Headspace Health Score: 2

How did you get on? Could you identify elements of yourself and your habits? Remember these 'foodie groups' are not designed to give you a fixed, permanent label. They are designed to help you identify your tendencies, your patterns of eating, your attitudes towards food, dieting and your body. The more you can notice these playing out in everyday life, the more aware you'll become of what it is you're doing, and why it is you're doing it. And with awareness comes choice. Indulge instinctively from a place of confusion, or refrain effortlessly from a place of clarity. But don't just limit this awareness to your own eating patterns, begin to notice how those around you eat as well. How do friends and family relate to food? What foodie group would you put them in? Seeing these different tendencies and behaviours in others can help to bring about a greater understanding and awareness within oneself.

CHAPTER FIVE

THE DYNAMICS OF BODY (DOUGHNUTS)

Although we spend all day with our bodies, thoughts and emotions, most of us know remarkably little about them. That's not altogether our fault, of course. If we are not taught about them at school, do not require a direct understanding of them for our work, and if no one ever encourages us to take a look, why would we bother? It's only when we have some vested personal interest that these things start to become more important to us. Now assuming you've bought this book for the reasons I think you have, then I guess the importance of our bodies, thoughts and emotions becomes more obvious in relation to our eating habits. Because, let's face it, eating doesn't happen by accident. The doughnut doesn't jump off the plate into your mouth. There is a process taking place. Of course usually it's all taking place so quickly that we don't get to notice what's actually happening.

But what if someone slowed down the tape a little; what if you saw that process clearly, at each and every stage? What if you became used to listening for those triggers and cues and were able to respond from a place of calm consideration? What if you were able to follow the journey from the moment of sensory impact, to the moment of consumption? Would it change the way you eat? Would it change the food choices you make? Would it influence your feelings towards the doughnut? My guess is that it would transform them forever. After all, this is exactly what it means to be mindful: to be aware, to listen to your thoughts and emotions, with a healthy sense of perspective and the ability to make skilful choices around food. With that in mind, let's rewind the tape to the very first moment.

AN INTRODUCTION TO THE SENSES

So, the doughnut is sitting there on a plate in the middle of a table. At what point does it grab your attention? Is it when you first turn and see it, admiring the perfect spherical ball of dough with its sugary sprinkles? Or was it when its sweet scent wafted in your direction? Maybe it was the sound of it being rattled in a box that gave you a clue as to what pleasures awaited? Or was it not until you got it into your hands or mouth that the juices start to flow? Whichever it was, it was thanks to the remarkable human sensory system.

The five physical senses (sight, hearing, smell, touch and taste) enable perception and interaction with our external environment. Dedicated areas of the brain then receive and interpret this data from the senses, allowing us to carry out actions such as eating. Every person has his or her own unique relationship with each of the senses – whilst some people are more used to engaging sight, others are more attuned to smell. This may well reflect the type of foodie you identified yourself as being in the last chapter, so take a moment to think which is *your* most active sense. When it comes to food, of course, there's a pretty good chance that *all* of the senses will be engaged in some way or another. Eating is an intensely sensory experience which is why, when the mind is untrained and things are not seen clearly, the thoughts and feelings we experience around food can appear so overwhelming. But in paying attention to the physical senses, in watching them, and in understanding how they work in more detail, we can start to become aware of the process of desire or craving at a much earlier stage. Let's get back to our doughnut to see how the different sense organs engage with our spongy friend (or nemesis, as it may be).

Sight

'Oh, I didn't realise we had doughnuts in the office today [wow they look amazing] . . . shouldn't really, what with the diet and all [yeah, right, diet-shmiet; just look at them]. I suppose one wouldn't hurt [one box that is . . . oh my god, and they have the sugar sprinkles on too]. No, no, after you, please [quick, before someone else comes] . . . oh, thank you . . .'

You see it, you want it, you eat it. That's the usual process, right? Sure, each of those things might be punctuated by brief moments of panic, justification or guilt, but seeing it, wanting it and eating it is the usual chain of events for most people (especially if you're a Gorger, Zombie, Binger or Comfort Eater). And that chain of events all began with the eyes, which tend to be the most dominant of the five physical senses.

When the eyes first make contact with the doughnut, strange as it may sound, there is not yet the realisation that it is a doughnut. For all you know, it could be a giant piece of broccoli.

The conscious recognition of what it is can only be made once the information has been sent to the visual cortex via the optic nerve and then up to the frontal cortex of the brain. This optic nerve is like a super-highway, allowing the visual information to travel to the visual cortex in the quickest possible time.

The next part of seeing is known as visual perception. This requires the help of the brain to process and interpret the information. And it is about much more than simple recognition. The eyes will also be helping to assess the brightness, size, distance, and possibly even the speed at which you will have to run across the room to reach the doughnut before somebody else does.

Hearing

'Yeah, sorry, I really must finish this email [wait a minute, what was that? I heard something] . . . yeah, it's urgent [that rattle, was that somebody taking another doughnut?] . . . apparently they need it right away [sounded like the box was almost empty] . . . yep, I'm on it [get the doughnut . . . no, email first . . . no, doughnut first . . . are those footsteps I can hear]?'

The auditory system has an extraordinary capacity for conveying information. At first glance it might be tempting to think it has very little impact on our eating habits, but what about that advert that urged you to buy the doughnut, the suggestion of a friend that persuaded you to try the new variety, or the sizzling sound of a fresh one cooking as you pass a shop one morning?

Let's suppose that you suddenly become aware of the sound of a doughnut cooking, whilst standing in a doorway waiting for someone. You might be checking your emails or messages on your phone, not even having noticed what shop was behind you. But that won't stop the ear from processing the sound of the doughnut cooking. That's the beauty of hearing – it can process sounds without even concentrating on the source that produces it. In fact, the ear continues to hear even whilst you're asleep.

The sizzling sound will first be 'collected' by the outer ear and then 'conducted' to the inner ear, via the eardrum and a collection of tiny bones called ossicles. The vibration in the air created by the sizzling sound is then carried into the winding passages of the ear canal, where it is finally acknowledged by the brain.

As with sight, the brain then needs to recognise the sound – through loudness, pitch and type – and interpret what it is listening to. Only once it has confirmed the sound by comparing it to the sound of a sizzling doughnut in the memory banks, will it begin to fire up another part of the brain which is associated with desire.

Smell

'Yeah, I couldn't agree more [what is that smell?] . . . yeah, absolutely, I think that's a great idea [is that fresh doughnuts I can smell?] . . . yeah I've thought about it a lot [it really is doughnuts I can smell!] . . . no, no I'm listening, I was just thinking about it [where is that coming from?]. Sure thing, of course . . . would you excuse me for a moment?'

The nose is responsible for collecting scents and odours and channelling them to the brain. It's hard to imagine another physical sense that is so integral to our relationship with food, since for most people smell accounts for at least 75 per cent of what they actually perceive as taste. (Take note the next time you have a cold.)

So, what's happening in the body as you walk into the supermarket and all of a sudden the smell of doughnuts (cunningly diverted from the bakery to the entrance) is thrust upon you? Well, lots of little smell receptors (connected to the olfactory nerve at the back of your nose), interact with the vapours in the air, and then transmit the sensation to a certain part of the brain.

Although the 'smell science jury' is still out on this one, it's generally thought that the brain then recognises the odour by matching it against a 'chemical map' which stores the memory of smells. Amazingly, this map is thought to be made up of just seven primary smells. And yet, *somehow*, it comes to the conclusion that it can 'smell' doughnuts. No two people smell in exactly the same way though, so whilst a doughnut may smell great to you, it might smell positively sickly to someone else.

Of all the senses, smell is arguably one of the most evocative and emotive. Take a moment to think of your favourite-smelling food, and then your least favourite. The smell memory is often so strong that it engages the same processes as it would if the food was present. Smells can even affect your mood, having obvious implications for us all, but especially those prone to emotional eating habits, such as the Comfort Eater.

Touch

'Oh no, I'm fine thanks, really. [please offer it to me again] . . . no really, I'm on a diet [please, please offer it to me one more time] . . . oh, ok then, if you insist [phew, thank goodness for that] . . . thanks [wow that feels soft, must be fresh this morning . . .

*still feels warm: bet it tastes amazing] . . . you're so persuasive.
I'm not even hungry . . .'*

Touch is the first of the five senses to develop and is integral to our relationship with food. I guess that's hardly surprising given that the lips, tongue and fingertips all make it in to the Top 5 most sensitive parts of the body (I'll leave it to your imagination what the other two are). In short, it's touch that allows us to experience the texture and the temperature of the doughnut, both in our hands and in our mouth.

As we pick up the doughnut, some of the four million specialised nerve cells and sensory receptors within the skin will be activated by the temperature, vibration and pressure of the doughnut (do doughnuts vibrate?). It's at this stage that we're collecting information on whether it's hard or soft, rough or smooth, heavy or light, hot or cold, wet or dry. This information is then transferred to the brain, via your spinal cord, where recognition and assessment is carried out (is it a doughnut or a bagel? Is it fresh or is it stale?). This message will be helping you to create a mental picture of the doughnut, which will then stimulate either desire or dislike. This in turn will inform your decision on whether to indulge or refrain (based on texture), to eat it now or to wait for it to cool down (based on temperature), and whether to pick up just one doughnut, or to take two (based on pressure, or perceived weight). Of course, if you're a Zombie, you'll usually miss most of this and eat it regardless.

Taste

*'Yeah, I'm really sorry, the bus was late [all right keep your hair
on] . . . didn't even have time to get breakfast, had to grab a
coffee and this doughnut instead [which tastes unbelievable by*

the way] . . . uhuh [so sweet] . . . uhuh [it's actually melting in my mouth] . . . uhuh [I can't hear a word you're saying, lalala-lalala . . .]'

When it comes to our appreciation and understanding of food (and not just of doughnuts), taste, or flavour, is arguably the most relevant of the five senses. But in many ways, our experience of taste is so interconnected with the other senses that it is difficult to talk about it in isolation. As I said, approximately 75 per cent of 'taste' comes from 'smell', and then there's touch, texture, temperature, and many other things to add to the mix.

But the moment you bite into the doughnut, the taste receptors on the tongue and in the roof of the mouth (otherwise known as taste buds) are made active. And as the saliva mixes with the ingredients, so the 'reception' of those taste buds is heightened. You might have as many as 10,000 of these taste buds in your mouth, each comprised of over 100 cells. In fact some superhuman tasters, literally known as 'super-tasters', have up to 20,000 taste buds, double the amount of taste buds that others typically have. That's a lot of doughnut tasting power and explains why many of them go on to become professional food and drink tasters (now *there's* a job).

Most people are familiar with the four basic taste groups: salty, sweet, bitter and sour. Generally speaking, you will experience each of these tastes on a specific part of the tongue. In reality, though, the taste buds are far more complex than this, and other possible taste groups include the strange-sounding 'umami' (a meaty taste found in fermented and aged foods, such as soy sauce and cheese), coolness (found in mint or eucalyptus), spiciness (found in chillies), fattiness (found in fatty foods), and dryness (found in unripe fruit). Whatever the taste is, once the sensory receptors have perceived the *type* of taste, they then fire that information up to the brain via three different cranial nerves, where it makes an educated guess as to what the food is, what it tastes like, and whether it's a good idea to continue eating it. Because each of us has a unique tasting palate, what tastes delicious to one person might see another reaching for a bucket. What's more, many tastes can actually *become* enjoyable, even if you didn't like them previously. (You might like to try out the exercise at the end of Chapter 6 if there's a particular food you just wish you could grow to like.) But for now, back to our doughnut . . .

AN INTRODUCTION TO THE BRAIN

Welcome to the engine room, the brain, where the doughnut data collected from the five physical senses meets up to be assessed, recognised, and acted upon (or not, as the case might be). Why should you want to eat a doughnut in the first place? What is it that drives you to the point of consumption? There are two systems at work: the first regulates your body's need for energy, and through a complex interaction of hormones, neuropeptides and neurotransmitters (in the gut and the brain), you are *made* to feel hungry, encouraging you to eat. The second is that you simply love eating doughnuts, and have created some kind of positive emotional association with them. It is not that you *need* the doughnut, but rather that you *want* it. This ability to override the physical needs of the body can get us into all kinds of trouble, and is covered in much more detail in the next chapter. For now, though, let's just assume that you actually *need* the doughnut to provide the body with more energy.

In order to let your brain know whether to eat or to stop eating, the body generates hormones which signal to a part of the brain known as the hypothalamus. This area of the brain works in a similar way to a thermostat, but instead of controlling the temperature, it regulates many of our basic bodily functions. (It also regulates our sleep-cycle and sexual urges.) When it comes to regulating the intake of food, the hypothalamus monitors our insulin and blood-sugar levels, telling us when to eat, and when to *stop* eating. When we are unaware of these signals, we will obviously tend to undereat or overeat. Typically, these signals haven't disappeared, it's just that the signals making us *want* food drown out the signals that tell us whether we *need* food. Mindfulness will help put us back in touch with these more subtle signals, creating a much stronger awareness of physical sensations.

But why would the physical body ever want to encourage us to eat more food than we need? Well, the short answer is that for most of man's time on this planet we were short of food. Because of this, we've evolved to experience pleasure at the sight of high-calorie foods such as doughnuts, because of their ability to sustain us for long periods of time. The problem, of course, is that food is no longer so scarce. So despite this abundance of food, our reward system doesn't recognise that, and still generates high levels of arousal, pushing us ever closer to eating the doughnut and storing the calories for later.

In many ways, food impacts the brain's reward system in a similar way to taking drugs, or participating in other potentially addictive types of behaviour. This addictive craving is not only played out within the thoughts and the emotions of the *mind*, but also in the workings of the *body*, with the physical release of a neurotransmitter called dopamine. Dopamine makes us want things, so when our brain registers the sight of the doughnut, dopamine is released, bringing a sense of craving. When we then eat the doughnut, experiencing pleasure as we do, the brain learns to want it even more, releasing even more dopamine the next time our sensory system comes into contact with the doughnut.

With each new cycle, the brain becomes increasingly sensitive to this kind of reward – so much so that other, more mundane pleasures that we used to enjoy start to pale in comparison. At the same time, we start to build up a tolerance to the dopamine release, so we need more and more to get the same hit as before. In the end, the pleasure may not be that great at all, but the desire has become so strong that – if we are unaware – we might well feel compelled to seek out more doughnuts to relieve the craving. Who would have thought that the simple act of eating a doughnut could be quite so complicated? But the more you begin to notice these different triggers, associations and sensations, the more calm and clarity you will have around food and so make decisions that are right for *you*.

AN INTRODUCTION TO THE STOMACH

In order to make these right decisions and regulate our eating in the best possible way, the 'hunger centre' in the brain (the hypothalamus), needs to listen very carefully to the signals from the body – especially from the stomach. Because when we've burned up all the food in our stomachs and our blood sugar becomes low, our stomach secretes a hormone called ghrelin that communicates to our hypothalamus to stimulate our appetite. In just the same way, as we're refuelling, fat tissues secrete a different hormone called leptin which signals to the hypothalamus to put the brakes on and to stop eating.

As effective and sophisticated as this system might be, the problem is that when we're hungrily chowing down on that tasty doughnut, the signals from this hormonal response simply aren't noticed.

Most scientists agree that it takes the brain something close to 20 minutes to recognise that the stomach is full. This might be accompanied by a familiar feeling of tightness around the middle (requiring a loosening of the belt or, in really serious cases, a change into a pair of elasticated trousers). It's for this reason that dieticians will often encourage people to chew more and eat more slowly, so that the stomach has the necessary time to feed back this information to the brain and prevent us from overeating. This is good advice, because apart from anything else it will actually aid digestion and allow you to get the full nutritional benefits from the food you're consuming.

However, when it comes to eating, 20 minutes is a surprisingly long time and this leaves us a window of opportunity in which some serious damage can be done. (Take the world-record-holder for eating hot dogs as an example. Mr Kobayashi, nicknamed 'the tsunami' for his ability to consume, once polished off 69 hot dogs in just 10 minutes!) Much of the overeating that is done falls well within the 20-minute 'fullness recognition' scenario, and so simply eating until your body feels full has its obvious drawbacks. However, once you begin to get more familiar with mindful eating, you will not need the stomach to be bursting at the seams in order to be aware of its fullness. By noticing these physical signals on a regular basis you will very quickly develop the ability to recognise when the stomach is 50 per cent full or 75 per cent full, rather than only noticing anything in excess of 100 per cent full.

THE EFFECTS OF MINDFULNESS AND MIND TRAINING ON THE BODY

At Headspace we try hard not to make too many promises, because everyone is different, and the results of training the mind may well be different for different people. However, it is often really difficult, as there is so much exciting research out there which demonstrates the amazing benefits of mindfulness and other similar mind-training techniques. So, without making any guarantees, and simply reporting on what scientists have discovered in clinical research, here are my favourite top 10 scientific findings related to training your mind, as well as your body, in discovering (or rediscovering) your ideal weight, shape and size. You can find the effects on the mind and the emotions in the following chapter.

1. Mindfulness increases the density of neurons in your hippocampus, a part of the brain associated with emotional stability. And as you'll know, emotional stability means healthier eating.

2. It increases the blood flow to your insula. This is the part of the brain associated with awareness of bodily sensations, such as feeling full during, or after, a meal.

3. It reduces the production of the stress hormone, cortisol. This makes it easier to hold on to lean muscle mass, whilst at the same time losing those unwanted fat stores.

4. It reduces blood pressure, which can significantly decrease the risk of heart disease.

5. It increases blood flow to your anterior cingulate cortex, your self-control hub in the brain. This reduces the likelihood of being overwhelmed by food cravings.

6. It increases the activity of your lateral prefrontal cortex, which is all about self-regulating and decision-making. This has been associated with making healthier food choices.

7. It reduces the symptoms of Irritable Bowel Syndrome (IBS). In fact, it has been shown to be over three times more effective than attending a regular IBS support group.

8. It strengthens your immune system, which can help you to feel and look your best. And the way you feel physically can dramatically change the way you think about your body.

9. It increases activity in your cerebellum, a part of the brain which regulates the speed, consistency and appropriateness of thoughts and emotions.

10. It increases the connectivity between different areas of the brain, increasing the efficiency and speed at which messages

get relayed from one part to the next . . . Are you listening Mr Kobayashi?

The body is a remarkable organism, with a sensory system that allows us to gather information about food in the most incredibly detailed way. But it is an organism that requires a delicate state of *balance* in order to stay healthy and well. So the more we can be aware of these signals, the more in tune with the body we'll become. It is by training the mind in this way, through the practice of mindfulness, that we can learn how to sit with our emotions and desires, without necessarily acting upon them. This gives us the potential to live as intended, whilst at the same time living in an environment that has overtaken our physiological evolution. This is not some kind of fluffy, intangible change, but rather physical, structural and lasting. This is change that begins to rewire your hard drive, changing patterns of behaviour that you might once have considered to be with you for life. It is *mindful awareness* and *mindful eating* which allows that change to happen.

Mindfulness will give you the opportunity to live at your natural weight, and at a size that allows you to feel comfortable, confident and at ease with your body.

You *know* what the body needs to function well. It needs a balanced diet of healthy, fresh and nutritionally rich foods. (If you're not sure what these are, then check out The Headspace Handy Guide to Nutrition in Chapter 10. Whatever foods you choose, eating small, regular, nutritionally rich meals and snacks, as recommended for the 10-Day Plan, will help you to create a feeling of satisfaction or satiety in the body. This will not only reduce your level of hunger, but will also help to stabilise the blood-sugar levels that usually have you reaching for the biscuit tin in the middle of the afternoon.

HEADSPACE EXERCISE: PLAYING WITH THE SENSES

Now you might be flicking through this book thinking that although mindful eating sounds like a great *idea*, the practice of it looks a bit too much like hard work. Don't worry: there's no reason why the experience of mindful eating can't be a little more playful. You might even like to make it a sensual experience to share with your partner (although probably not on a first date, and probably not in a restaurant either). But before you go getting all *9½ Weeks* on me (if you're old enough to remember that 80s classic), it's worth remembering that mindfulness is about *not* getting swept away by emotions and thereby being able to rest in the present moment with an underlying sense of calm and clarity. In terms of eating, that means having clarity in making the choices that are best for *you*. Just something to think about as you put the chocolate sauce and whipped cream back in the fridge. Here's a short exercise for you to try. You will need a friend or partner for this one.

1. Sit down on a chair with an eye mask or blindfold on.

2. Ask your friend or partner to find 10 different foods from around the kitchen. It's best if they do this without your guidance and without taking your preferences into

account. Ask them to serve up mouthful-sized portions of each food and place them on a plate in front of you. (I'm sure it goes without saying, but ensure that the foods are cleaned and prepared in a way that makes them safe to eat.)

3. Next, ask them to guide your hand to the plate, and select one of the foods to taste. If you prefer (and you're feeling trusting), you can even get them to guide your hand towards a specific food on the plate. Either way, you should now have a piece of food in your hands.

4. Take your time to explore the food with your hands, giving a running commentary of what you can feel to the other person. This will encourage you to be much more thorough than you would be if you were describing it to yourself. Take time to notice the texture and the temperature, and see how the mind immediately projects an image of how you *think* it looks, even though you're unable to see it.

5. Now pass the food back to the other person and place your hands in your lap. Having already taken away the sense of sight to help you focus, you are now taking away the sense of touch, enabling you to focus even more intently on the flavours, sounds and smells.

6. Ask the other person to move the food towards your nose and hold it in place so you can sniff it. Try inhaling

deeply, with long, slow breaths, and then taking shorter, sharper breaths to pick up every possible smell. Many processed foods have surprisingly little smell, so you'll have to be especially alert if there are lots of E numbers involved.

7. Next, ask them to hold it right beside your ear and, if possible, to break a piece off. If that's *not* possible, then ask them to shake it around, run their fingers through it, or to somehow create some noise with it. This is likely to be more difficult than the other parts of the exercise and you'll really need to be listening carefully.

8. And now for the fun part. Ask them to *gently* place the food on your tongue. Allow the food to rest on the tongue for a moment to see what flavours you can pick up. You can then close your mouth and begin to move it around with the tongue, noticing which flavours are most obvious. Where in the mouth do you experience them? The back, the front, the roof of the mouth, the side of the tongue? Take the time to notice.

9. If you can, be aware of what thoughts meet the food as you taste it. For example, is there a feeling of pleasure or disappointment? Is there a feeling of predictability or surprise? Does the mind immediately go into overdrive, craving more of the food, or do you find yourself craving mouthwash to get rid of the taste?

10. Finally, take the time to notice any particularly strong emotional reactions. For example, does the food bring about a sense of comfort and security, or does it make you feel anxious, guilty or uncertain? Try to get a sense of what emotional triggers are in play for each of these foods. You can then swap over with the other person and let them have a go at the exercise too.

CHAPTER SIX

THE DYNAMICS OF MIND
(CHOCOLATE)

Having looked at the processes at work in the *body*, you might be tempted to blame your eating habits on your hypothalamus for not regulating your system correctly, or perhaps your dopamine reward system for dishing out more reward than you actually need. But that would be a mistake. (Apart from anything else, this is not about looking to blame some*thing* or some*one* for the way that we are, but rather an investigation into *why* we do the things we do.)

Because, in addition to the strong physical and chemical reactions taking place in the body, there is also the influence of thought and feeling taking place in the mind. What is it that drives you to pick up that bar of chocolate, even when the body doesn't need it? Is it a thought, or is it a feeling? Or are the two things indistinguishable? Do you do it because you 'think' it's a good idea, even though you don't 'feel' like it, or do you just 'feel' like it, even though you 'think' it's a bad idea? When it comes to the human mind, it's often difficult for us to separate thought and feeling.

AN INTRODUCTION TO THOUGHT

The words 'brain' and 'mind' are often used interchangeably, and many people tend to think of them as the same thing. However, there is a big difference in both the appearance and the way in which the two are experienced. As you are picturing that chocolate bar, where is it? Does it appear as though the picture is being projected in front of you? Can you touch it? Is it something solid and tangible? Or is it something spacious and *intangible*? Now, unless you have the ability to conjure up chocolate bars out of thin air (wouldn't that be sweet?), I'm assuming that what you will have found is . . . well, nothing. Strange as that may sound, when we look at a thought in this way, we see that there is nothing there. It's as though we can put our hand right through it.

And yet, there is *something* there, isn't there? After all, you can see it, it makes you feel a certain way, it might even remind you of the smell or the taste of the chocolate bar. In this way a thought is a bit like a rainbow or a cloud. Because on the one hand, a rainbow is bright, vivid and clearly visible to the naked eye, but on the other hand (as anyone other than a leprechaun will tell you), you can chase the rainbow all you like, but you will never be able to reach the end of it, because there is no inherent substance to it. And the mind is much the same. When a thought appears in the mind, regardless of whether it has arrived of its own volition, or you've conjured it up, it lacks real substance. However, whilst a thought might be empty in nature, it is nonetheless packed full of chocolate thinking *potential.*

THE PROCESS

So, you're sitting there writing an email, when all of a sudden a thought pops into the mind, 'I could do with some chocolate.' You didn't *consciously* bring the thought to mind, it just came out of nowhere, right? Maybe it was stimulated by a sound, a smell, a memory, or association, but whatever the trigger was, you suddenly found yourself thinking 'I could really do with some chocolate.' This is an interesting moment in time, because this is the moment of potential. And, as we all know, when it comes to inner dialogue, the potential can go in any direction.

Potential A: Indulgence

'I could really do with some chocolate . . . maybe get one of those new chocolate caramel bars . . . I can almost taste it . . . maybe finish the email first . . . no, it can wait; besides, the extra sugar will help me to concentrate . . . Maybe I should buy two of them, just in case I get this urge later as well . . . I could always keep one in my desk drawer for another time. Yeah, right . . . like that'll stay there for more than an hour . . . OK, so maybe I buy three bars instead . . . '

Potential B: Resistance

'I could really do with some chocolate . . . NO! Don't think about it . . . go away – carrot sticks, carrot sticks, carrot sticks . . . Nope, I'm not listening, I'm not going to give in . . . *please* don't let me give in . . . lalalalalala . . . oh, why won't you just leave me alone? I don't want any chocolate . . . OK, so I do . . . but I'm not going to have any because I know it makes me look fat . . .

121

God, I hate the way I look . . . please don't make me eat another chocolate bar . . . '

Potential C: Mindfulness

'I could really do with some chocolate . . . oh look, a thought.'

What usually happens when we see a thought in the mind is that we react to it. In *reacting*, we give it momentum. It might be forward momentum, as in Potential A, or reverse momentum, as in Potential B. Either way, the knee-jerk reaction (which often happens outside of our awareness) leads to a chain of thought that has the potential to result in an action we might later regret (like polishing off a family-sized box of chocolates all on our own). Funnily enough, even Potential B, where there is lots of resistance, can still lead to us buying the chocolate bar. That's because it is often as a *result* of this resistance and the inner conflict that it creates that we decide to throw in the towel, just to get a little peace of mind.

You've probably already noticed that the inner dialogue for Potential C is very brief. This is best-case scenario, of course, but assuming you are being mindful and aware, then when that first thought arises, you see it clearly, knowing that just like the rainbow it is empty, nonexistent, yet all the same bursting with potential. In seeing it clearly, the thought loses its momentum and dissolves into thin air. There is no indulgence in the thought, and so no additional forward momentum, and there is no resistance to the thought, so there is no 'pent-up' or reverse momentum. There is simply a thought that appears and then disappears.

Of course, it may well take a little practice to become aware of the first thought so quickly, or to see it so clearly, remembering that it has no power over you when seen in this context. But as you know now, mindfulness (and mindful eating) is a skill. It requires practice, both in the form of taking a short period of time out each day to get familiar with this sense of awareness (like the Take10 exercise in the next chapter), but also in remembering to be more aware in daily life. The great thing is, as you remember to be more aware, so the feeling of awareness becomes more familiar. And in becoming more familiar, it becomes that much easier to remember to be aware: a virtuous circle of awareness.

Now there are undoubtedly physical prompts that lead to those 'first thoughts' arising, and the more we understand the origin of those triggers, the more awareness we're likely to apply to the thoughts and behaviour that they encourage. Let's take a look at some of the likely candidates for prompting uninvited chocolate thoughts.

THE TRIGGERS

Environment

'I love going to fill the car up with petrol . . . I always treat myself with a bar of . . . '

What do you buy to eat every time you go to the cinema? What about every time you go to the airport or the train station? What do you tend to eat at work? Our environment can very easily trigger thoughts and, for many people, simply walking towards the freezer will stimulate the thought of ice cream. Likewise, being in a pub might stimulate the thought of buying a bag of crisps or nuts. What foods do you associate with what places?

Activity

'I can't wait to watch this movie . . . better get the chocolate before I sit down though . . .'

What's the first thought that pops into your mind when you plonk yourself down in front of the TV? For many people it will be 'Hmmm, maybe I should have something to eat.' This is a strong association that may well see you hopping straight back out of the chair to get something to 'keep you company' whilst you watch whatever's on the box. This is equally true when we're driving or travelling, hanging out with certain groups of friends, and especially when cooking or preparing food.

Company

'I love catching up with Mum . . . she always has some chocolate with her . . .'

Do you eat certain types of food with certain types of people? For example, will sitting down for a cup of tea with your mum stimulate a thought about homemade cake? Or will sitting on the sofa with a partner stimulate the thought of takeaway? And do you tend to eat more when you're with others? Very often it is other people and associations with them that will prompt food-related thoughts to arise.

Physical Sensations

'Wow I feel tired . . . maybe a bar of chocolate would pick me up a little bit . . .'

Although intimately connected to the senses, this one has more to do with general feelings of lethargy, stress, discomfort, pain, hormonal fluctuations, or any of the physical sensations related to hunger – such as a painful stomach. It's amazing how quickly the thought can be stimulated in these situations. Even the slightest twinge in the stomach can trigger a thought of food. Or it might be a feeling of tiredness, caused by low blood-sugar levels that triggers the thought.

Sensory Contact

'That chocolate smells so good . . . . I'm going to have to buy some too . . . '

As I mentioned in the last chapter, the senses are incredibly adept at picking up information from our surroundings. And because food plays such an important role in life, it's no co-incidence that food-related thoughts, triggered by the senses, are happening left, right and centre. Think about it, is there any way you can walk down a busy street without experiencing thoughts about food? Whether it's the sight of something in a shop window, the sound of hot dogs cooking on a street stand, or the smell of cakes from a bakery, they are all likely to stim-ulate food-related thoughts. Sometimes, much like a Zombie, we'll just follow the sense to the point of consumption.

Emotional Highs

'Can't believe I passed my driving test . . . think I'll have some chocolate to celebrate . . . '

It's been a fantastic day and you feel great. Does the thought of celebrating with a treat pop into your mind? You are madly in love and want to spend the evening with your loved one. Do you think about going out (or staying in) for dinner? It is not just the so-called 'negative' emotions that trigger thoughts for food: pleasant feelings can just as easily stimulate these thoughts.

125

Emotional Lows

'I hate the way I look and that diet didn't work – maybe some chocolate will cheer me up . . . '

Let's say you're feeling a little blue. Does that ever trigger the thought for food? What about when you're feeling anxious? Do the butterflies in the stomach trigger a thought about food (even if it's aversion)? And how about if you feel lonely? Does that ever trigger a food-related thought? When it comes to challenging emotional states, the associations between the temporary alleviation of that emotion and food can be incredibly strong. This will be especially apparent if you have a tendency to eat in a similar way to a Comfort Eater or a Binger.

The Clock

'Great, it's almost 3pm . . . chocolate-o'clock time . . . '

'Oh, it's one o'clock, I'd better have something to eat.' 'Ten to eleven . . . only ten minutes until coffee and biscuits.' They are nothing but two hands on a round disc of numbers, yet the clock can stimulate thoughts about food like nothing else. Usually this is tied in to the importance of meal times when we were younger, or is linked to anticipated rewards (back to that dopamine system again) based on a work-time vs free-time calculation.

Other Substances

'I really need some chocolate . . . I've got to get some . . . have you got any chocolate?'

Do you have a strong association between wine and nibbles, or a pint and pork scratchings? And what about when you've really drunk a lot? Does that trigger the thought of a doner kebab? Some substances are so intertwined with creating a desire for food that they've inspired phrases, such as – with cannabis – 'to get the munchies'. Hardly likely to affect the Gourmet this one, but definitely one for the Socialite to watch out for.

THE HABIT OF THOUGHT

We tend to assume that our appetites are defined by the way food *tastes*, but as you can see from the triggers, the environmental and emotional associations are often far more likely to prompt habitual thought than the tastes themselves. In fact, in a recent study at the University of Southern California, researchers served up cold, spongy, week-old popcorn to people going to the movies. And to everyone's surprise, they ate every bit as much as those lucky enough to get the fresh stuff. *That* is the power of habitual thought. The research suggests that once we've *formed* an eating habit, we don't even care what the food *tastes* like. Not only that, but if the impulse and association is strong enough, we'll eat the same amount, no matter whether it's fresh or stale, new or old. Simply having that environmental association and experiencing that familiar thought is enough to get us to follow through with the action of eating.

So, if we're willing to eat soggy old popcorn simply because the thought pops into our head every time we walk in through the doors of the cinema, then just imagine how many other areas of life we might be applying a similar attitude towards. Take a moment to think back to the *process* of thought, where we have that moment of potential. You'll remember that in that moment we have the opportunity to be mindful, to see the thought clearly, or to drift into indulgence or resistance.

Let's say that the pattern of thought develops through a desire for the chocolate bar, so a tendency to get involved in indulgence. I think the easiest way to think about this is to imagine the thoughts as links in a chain. The first thought (the one about chocolate) is like the first link in a chain. But without any other links to join it, it has not even become a chain, it is simply a link. At this stage it has no momentum whatsoever, and so if it is seen clearly, it simply falls away. But what *usually* happens is that we miss that first thought, that first link. It is as though it happens outside of our awareness, with every new thought adding more links to the chain. Now, if we are *really* unaware, really *unmindful*, then we might not even notice until the chain is 5 or 10 minutes long (that's a lot of links in the chain). It's at this point you suddenly realise that you have been daydreaming about chocolate for all that time, and have followed the thought through so completely that (in your mind) you have walked to the shop, bought it, eaten it, regretted it, gone on a diet, felt good about yourself, and then gone and bought another bar of chocolate. Such is the tendency for the mind to wander.

The problem is, by this stage the chain of thought is running at such speed and with so much momentum that it is highly likely that we will follow the thought through to the point of action (the point at which we actually pick up the chocolate bar and eat it). This is in no small part due to all the physiological signals and processes that are beginning in the body as we imagine eating the chocolate. And the more often we allow the mind to wander off in this way, the more often we stimulate those same chemical response patterns, and the stronger the tendency becomes to travel that same route. In short, we develop a habitual pattern of thought. This in turn is reflected in the patterns of the brain, where specific neural pathways are formed and strengthened every time you have that series of thoughts. It's as though you are creating a super-highway of chocolate-induced thought. The more times you use the highway, the more defined it becomes, and the more defined it becomes, the more you use the highway. At best this can be a slightly frustrating pattern; at worst it has the potential to be incredibly destructive.

THE IMPLICATIONS OF BEING MINDFUL OF THOUGHT

Now I appreciate that these ideas may be a little hard to grasp – that tends to be the way when discussing matters of the mind. That's why the practicality of the next chapter is so important. But broadly speaking, listening to thoughts happens as soon as we start to apply the technique of mindfulness. It means stepping back from the busy-ness of the mind, and instead viewing thoughts from a place of awareness and perspective. Seeing thoughts clearly means knowing how to achieve and maintain a balanced and generally calm state of mind, so that you can remain focused but relaxed in witnessing the thoughts and feelings of the mind. Relating to thoughts with sensitivity means not criticising or judging the thoughts that you see, instead meeting them with empathy, understanding, patience and compassion. As for letting thoughts go without attachment and resistance, this means letting go of the urge to do battle with the mind on the one hand, and not getting carried away with particular thoughts or feelings on the other.

This is a place of quiet equanimity, of happy contentment, where you consciously allow thoughts to come and go, without the need to suppress so-called negative thoughts, or encourage so-called positive thoughts. It is *not* about thinking, persuading, reasoning, justifying or conceptualising. Neither is it about willpower. It is about *awareness*, the natural intelligence of the mind, enabling you to see the thought so clearly that you feel no compulsion to act on it (unless you want to, of course). This experience is so ordinary, and yet so *extra*ordinary at the same time. It is *ordinary* because it requires so little effort, because it is naturally arising, because it is nothing but the natural intelligence of your own mind. It is *extraordinary* because it puts choice back into your own hands. It's like taking off a blindfold and seeing things clearly, as you've never seen them before.

More than that, though, it gives you the space and freedom you need to make the right decisions for *you*. It is this new-found sense of calm and clarity that is going to help you come to a place where you are happy and content with how you look and feel. Rather than *reacting*, habitually, to thoughts, feelings and situations around food, it will give you the space to breathe. It will give you the time to *respond* in a new way, to consider what's best for you, unaffected by the usual conflicting, confusing or overwhelming emotions. As you can imagine, when it comes to making the right dietary choices and having a healthy relationship with your body, the difference between an instinctive reaction and a considered response is everything.

AN INTRODUCTION TO EMOTIONS

Just as with thought, for something that's so central to our entire experience of life, we have remarkably little understanding of our emotions. That's usually because we're so wrapped up in them that we can't get the necessary perspective to see them clearly. Of course, neuroscientists can now tell us what's happening physiologically (to our brain) when we experience an emotion, and behavioural scientists can see how emotions affect our behaviour. And this is all very helpful – but does it change the way you feel? More importantly, does it change the way you *react* to the way you feel? Because, just as with thought, we may *know* the intellectual arguments about the different qualities of emotion, but that alone doesn't change our *experience* of them.

For example, you may know that you 'shouldn't' get angry with yourself for eating the chocolate bar (because that anger releases harmful hormones into your body and causes your blood pressure to rise), but that knowledge does little to stop you getting angry. Likewise, you may know that taking it easy and being a bit more carefree with your diet will make you feel less stressed, but that information is of little use if you're going out of your mind with worry about what you're eating. This gap between what we know and understand *intellectually*, and our actual *experience* of emotions in everyday life, can often appear as an enormous chasm. In this way, mindfulness can be considered the bridge between these two different types of knowledge, leading to a more genuine understanding of the emotions and a more definable shift in our behaviour.

Of course, emotional triggers and patterns of behaviour are part of being human. As long as we are alive, these feelings are likely to play out in the mind, and to attempt to prevent or 'get rid' of the emotions will cause all kinds of problems. 'Feeling' emotions is part of being human, a very *necessary function* of being human. Funnily enough, it's not usually the emotion itself that is the problem, but rather the way we react to it and relate to it. And as you will have already guessed, the trick is to learn how to step back from it all, to identify the emotion when it first arises, watch it as it unfolds and washes over you, and then simply let it go. This is the practice of mindfulness. It is learning to take up a position where you *see* the emotion clearly, *feel* the emotion clearly, from a place of calm, no longer feeling the need to suppress or indulge that feeling. From this place of awareness, emotions are spectacular rather than terrifying, and transformative rather than destructive.

Although this concept is simple and straightforward enough, as you can imagine it takes a little practice to be able to let go of emotions effortlessly. That's why a consistent and regular mindfulness practice is so important. One of the many benefits of the Take10 exercise in the next chapter is that it shows you how to become more aware of your emotions. It shows you how to become familiar with them, how to allow them space to breathe, and how to take them a little less seriously (without undermining the importance of the trigger). So, Take10 will undoubtedly provide the best framework for you to come to know your emotions well.

THE PROCESS

Is there anything in life that is *not* influenced by our emotions? They affect our perception of people (including ourselves), of situations, our life circumstances and the environment in which we live. They are nothing less than the filter between 'us' and the 'world' (between 'you' and 'the chocolate bar'). As a result, they colour and define our every experience of life. If you've ever owned a pair of sunglasses with tinted lenses then you'll know that when you put them on, it immediately changes your perspective of everything around you. It's as if everything takes on the tinted appearance of the coloured lens. Nothing around you has changed, but the way in which you *view* it is different.

Emotions work in a similar way. When we feel angry the world can look like a very threatening place, and certain foods can look like a very comforting alternative, or a welcome distraction. In this particular state of mind we tend to see situations as obstacles, and other people (or even ourselves) as bad guys. This is what the world looks like when we see it through an angry lens. Yet when we feel happy, the world looks positively different. We see the same situations as opportunities and the same people (possibly ourselves) as good guys. This is what it looks like through the 'happy lens'. The world around us hasn't changed that much, but our experience of that world is radically different.

As with thought, there is a moment of potential that exists with emotion – and that exists in the very first moment that we realise, or become aware, that we're feeling a certain way.

Potential A: Indulgence of the Emotion

'Oh, I didn't realise I was feeling anxious . . .

' . . . well, it's hardly surprising is it . . . I can't believe I've put on more weight. How could that have possibly happened? I've been eating like a bird . . . and I've got the holiday coming up. I'm never going to fit in to my bikini . . . I'm going to look like a whale . . . this is going to be so humiliating. How am I ever going to lose enough weight . . . maybe I'm destined to be fat . . . maybe I should stop going on beach holidays . . . maybe just go skiing instead . . . '

Potential B: Resistance of the Emotion

'Oh, I didn't realise I was feeling anxious . . .

' . . . Oh no, I'm feeling anxious again. I hate feeling this way . . . quick, think lots of positive thoughts . . . I'm not anxious, I'm not anxious, I'm not anxious . . . oh my god I still feel anxious . . . How can I get rid of this feeling? I've got no reason to feel anxious . . . it's all in my head . . . I know it's all in my head . . . so why can't I get rid of it? Oh, I hate this feeling . . . how do I get rid of it? . . . '

Potential C: Mindfulness

'Oh, I didn't realise I was feeling anxious . . .

' . . . that's interesting . . . OK, so what is the actual experience of anxiety? What is the physical sensation? What is the . . . hey, where did the anxiety go?'

As you can see, this moment of potential can play out in a number of different ways, depending on our level of awareness, and how we tend to react to that particular emotion. What often surprises people when it comes to emotions is that a strong *resistance* to an emotion tends to lead to just as much mental unrest as indulgence – arguably more. Whichever it is, both indulgence and resistance are like fuel for the fire, and will almost inevitably keep the flames of that particular emotion burning bright. Mindfulness, on the other hand, brings about and encourages a slightly more spacious and objective approach, which can radically alter this process – as you saw from the example. The emotion may not disappear immediately, but as long as we meet it with a gentle, friendly and curious attitude, then we will be using the opportunity to see the emotion for what it really is, rather than being afraid or annoyed at what we think it *might* be.

Over time, observing the emotions in this way weakens their hold over us. They no longer appear as frightening, overwhelming or debilitating. Instead they provide us with an opportunity to know our own mind and to live life well. In some ways the process of emotion is similar to the relationship with thoughts. Because it is only when we become aware of how we are feeling that we can consciously let go of it. When we become caught up in the emotion, we 'become' that emotion. So, if there is loneliness, then 'I will be lonely' and therefore 'I'm going to eat because I'm lonely'. This is quite different to seeing the emotion *clearly*, with a different perspective, and perhaps a greater sense of 'Oh, there's a lot of loneliness around today.' It may sound like a very subtle difference, but it is such a profound shift of perspective that it can change your life in a way that you may never have thought possible.

THE TRIGGERS

The triggers for establishing the onset of an emotion can be as wide-ranging as the triggers for stimulating a thought. However, what's more interesting, in this context, is to look at how these emotional triggers then lead to certain *behaviour* around food. For example, what are your eating habits when you feel sad? And what about when you feel angry, or anxious? Does food simply become 'something to do' when you feel bored? How about the deeper states of loneliness, guilt and self-loathing, which can so often trigger bouts of emotional eating?

And it's not just the so-called negative emotions that can act as emotional triggers. Take the feeling of excitement. Do you tend to get carried away with *how much* you eat or *what* you eat when you feel that way? And what about when you just feel very happy? Is that an emotional cue that signals all is well in the world and that a slice of pizza would simply be the icing on the cake (or the cheese on the pizza)?

Look at the following list of emotions and consider how they affect your own personal eating habits. Do they encourage you to eat more or less frequently? More or less healthily? And do they result in you eating more or less food? These questions and this type of reflection is important in understanding your eating habits and will play an important part in your 10-Day Plan. You might find it useful to write down the answers for each emotion in the spaces provided below.

The Dynamics of Mind (Chocolate)

1. Excited

Typical reaction:

Increase or decrease in food consumed:

2. Depressed

Typical reaction:

Increase or decrease in food consumed:

3. Anxious

Typical reaction:

Increase or decrease in food consumed:

4. Happy

Typical reaction:

Increase or decrease in food consumed:

5. Angry

Typical reaction:

Increase or decrease in food consumed:

6. Content

Typical reaction:

Increase or decrease in food consumed:

7. Exhausted

Typical reaction:

Increase or decrease in food consumed:

8. Guilty

Typical reaction:

Increase or decrease in food consumed:

9. Supported

Typical reaction:

Increase or decrease in food consumed:

10. Lonely

Typical reaction:

Increase or decrease in food consumed:

THE HABIT OF EMOTION

The process that leads to emotional eating is entirely normal. As I said in the Introduction, there are few people in the developed world, living above the poverty line, who eat out of hunger alone. Almost everyone is susceptible to these emotional triggers and patterns. In fact, they are likely to be some of the most deep-rooted, conditioned responses that we experience in life. A recent US study found that fully 100 per cent of the women interviewed in a random study looking at food addiction reported experiencing occasional craving for food, as did 70 per cent of men. It is this same emotional craving that can feel so overwhelming to us all at times.

Emotional eating is only really a problem when it becomes your main strategy for regulating mood on a frequent basis. This habit of behaviour might be a conscious plan, or something that you 'simply do' without being aware of it at all. Whichever it is, the reason I say it becomes a 'problem' is that it tends to result in unhealthy behaviour. For example, it's quite common to adopt a pattern of binging when you are involved in habits of emotional eating. In fact it's estimated that well over 10 per cent of the population – male and female – regularly indulges in binging.

As a rule, the stronger the habitual tendency, the more likely we will follow through with some kind of action. Once again, it's important to consider the flipside too. When we have a strong resistance to a particular tendency, *that* resistance is likely to be every bit as powerful (even if the potential lies dormant). For example, have you ever been strict with your eating, perhaps living with a degree of self-loathing, only to blow the lid one day and indulge in lots of junk food? The strength of that blow-out will have been equal to the degree of self-loathing. Much as we say 'I won't, I can't, I mustn't', we will at the same time be nurturing a sense of 'I will, I can, I must'. These things are simply two sides of the same coin. The more you strengthen the one, the more you strengthen the potential for the other. This is why willpower alone is never enough to cause any lasting, sustainable change in behaviour around food.

In many ways this is expressed best in the mentality of a

yo-yo dieter, or the Diet Junkie, who is very strict, then very loose, and then very strict again. As you can probably imagine (or might even be able to testify), under normal circumstances it can be hard to escape this pattern of behaviour, to step back from the often overwhelming swings of emotion. That's where the third potential becomes so relevant: not indulging the emotion, not resisting the emotion, but stepping back and seeing the emotion clearly with mindful awareness.

This is a skill that anyone can learn, it just takes a little practice. Funnily enough, it's sometimes thought that if we listen too much to the emotions, and operate from a place of gentle understanding rather than militant dominance, we will never achieve our goals. In fact many of us are hard-wired to believe that we need to *convince* ourselves to feel differently, or *force* ourselves to change. However, new research is showing just the opposite. At Wake Forest University in the US, they recently found that by cultivating an accepting and compassionate attitude towards ourselves, we can actually *reduce* our level of craving and comfort eating. The psychologists asked 84 women, many of whom were dieting, to eat a doughnut. Straight afterwards they were asked to eat a sweet. After that, they could then either stop eating altogether, or continue eating as many sweets as they wanted. The women were split into two equal-sized groups: one group who had been taught how to be more compassionate and kind towards themselves, and one group who had not received any such guidance.

What they found was that the women who'd been taught to be compassionate to themselves, who gave themselves permission to eat the sweets, ate significantly less than the other group. At the same time, those who were berating themselves and distraught at having already eaten a doughnut, actually ended up eating more. The research shows that very often self-criticism actually ends up fuelling our negative eating patterns, rather than halting them. On the other hand, when we go easy on ourselves, and are therefore less emotionally reactive, we become less stressed, and less likely to comfort eat.

This is a fascinating study and one that has clear implications for weight loss – not to mention the way we approach our habitual emotional states. Denial simply increases the chances of us losing it one day and undoing all the hard work. Whereas permission gives us a sense of freedom and spaciousness in which we don't necessarily feel compelled to act upon every little whim or desire. It's probably worth mentioning that those high in self-compassion have also been found to be more resilient, more socially connected and less prone to anxiety and depression.

THE EFFECTS OF MINDFULNESS ON THE EMOTIONS

Mindfulness has been shown to be particularly effective in creating change in emotional patterns. In one study, 'large' binges were reduced by 70 per cent and 'regular' binges by 50 per cent after a 42-day mindfulness programme centred around eating. Again the levels of depression and anxiety that participants reported feeling prior to the study also dropped from clinical to subclinical levels by the end of it.

In a separate study at the University of California, researchers found that those people who engaged in emotional eating, typically struggled to identify, regulate and manage their emotions. But with the introduction of regular mindfulness practice, they discovered that the technique helped to unravel this condition. They concluded that 'By being mindful, we learn to eat in a more relaxed, nonjudgemental way, more aware of our emotions, more aware of our appetite, when we need to eat, and when we need to stop.' This is a really interesting point, because very often mindfulness is presented as a way of 'dampening down' the emotions, of becoming emotionally numb. But what the researchers have found is that rather than becoming *less* aware of emotions, the practice of mindfulness actually makes you *more* aware of emotions. The difference is perspective. So, rather than being *involved* in the emotion, rather than *becoming* the emotion, there is the ability to observe the emotion, with no need to suppress or indulge. Doesn't that sound like a sane way to eat, a sane way to live?

THE EFFECTS OF MINDFULNESS AND MIND TRAINING ON THE MIND

As I said, when looking at the effects of mindfulness and mind training on the body, these findings are not promises or guarantees of what will happen immediately, as each of us is different. However, they *are* reflective of results found in scientific clinical trials and so there is no reason at all why you shouldn't experience the same benefits. Whereas some of these studies were run over the course of just five days or a week, many more lasted much longer than that – usually around eight weeks. Here's my own top 10 favourite findings for being inspired to train your mind as well as your body in discovering (or rediscovering) your ideal weight, size and shape.

1. It reduces the urge to binge or comfort eat, with *reduced* reactivity in the part of the brain associated with compulsion, and *increased* activity in the area associated with self-control.

2. It reduces mind wandering, which can often lead to 'unconscious decision-making' around food. But if your mind doesn't wander, then you can be conscious of the decision instead.

3. It reduces the *intensity* of emotion. For example, in becoming consciously aware of 'desire', and acknowledging it, the mind settles down, making it less likely to act it out.

4. It significantly reduces the incidence of habitual behaviour around food, as mindfulness has been shown to help rewire the neural circuits that encourage their tendency.

5. It can improve sleep quality and reduce insomnia, halving the time it takes people to go to sleep. Given that healthy sleep patterns are so closely linked to obesity, this is incredibly important.

6. It reduces feelings of anxiety (about food, the body and everything else). In fact many studies have shown that it *significantly* reduces the level of anxiety. Wouldn't that be nice?

7. It reduces addictive tendencies and behaviour. In fact, it has been shown to be more effective at helping people give up smoking than any other drug-free treatment in the US.

8. It reduces recurring bouts of depression (for those with three or more prior episodes). It has even been shown to be as effective as antidepressants for this.

9. It increases awareness of your thoughts and allows you to experience emotions more fully, and with greater understanding. This means making the food choices that are right for you.

10. It increases feelings of happiness, wellbeing and optimism. It's hard to overstate the importance of these things in living a healthy life and enjoying a sustainable eating plan.

HEADSPACE EXERCISE: UNDERSTANDING LIKES AND DISLIKES

Have you ever wondered why you like some foods, but dislike others? I want you to make a list right now in the back of this book of your top three 'most loved' foods and your top three 'most unloved' foods. What is it about those three foods you don't like? Is it the taste, the texture, the smell, the sound as you eat it, or the way it looks? Write the reasons down if you find it easier. Maybe it has nothing to do with any of those things. Perhaps it's because you've been told that it's bad for you, because it's unhealthy in some way. Or maybe it's do with an association between the food and certain time and place in your life – or even a certain person in your life. And of course the same applies to all those foods that you just can't get enough of. Whether it is because of your senses, or an emotional association, there is a good reason you like it.

In developing a strong and steady mindfulness practice, there is something fundamentally useful in the investigation of these likes and dislikes. This doesn't mean analysing your past or going into therapy, but simply developing a curious attitude to your likes, dislikes and eating habits. You've probably guessed where this is heading, and in the interests of developing a new relationship with food and your body, I can't recommend the two following exercises enough. Remember, this is between you and yourself, so there's no pressure to eat something you really dislike with a passion (and please don't eat anything that you are allergic to). Likewise, I'm not encouraging you to gorge on foods you really enjoy.

Exercise 1: *Foods You Like*

1. Take a food that you really like and sit down at a table with it.

2. What's the first thing that comes into your mind when you look at it? What is it that appeals? No matter what it is, continue to examine each of the following points, keeping in mind what it was that first came to mind.

3. Is it the way it *looks*? And if it is, what is it about the way it looks that engages you? Is it the packaging, the colour of the food, the shape or the design? Pick it up and have a closer look.

4. Is it the *smell* of the food? If it is, what is it about the

smell that attracts you? Is it the sweetness, the spiciness or the saltiness of the food? Again, pick it up, smell it and try to understand what it is that you like so much.

5. Is it the *texture* of the food? If it is, what is it about the texture that you like? Is it the feel or the temperature of the food that you like when it's in front of you? Or is it the memory of how it feels when it's in your mouth? Maybe it's the crunchy sensation you enjoy or the soft melting feeling.

6. Is it the *sound* of the food? If it is, what is it about the sound that excites you? Is it the rustle of a packet, the crisp snap as you break something in half, or is it the sound of the food continuing to cook after it's come out of the oven?

7. Is it the *taste* of the food? And of course this is the one you've been waiting for. If it is the taste, then what is it about the taste that draws you in? Is it the sweetness, the saltiness, the spiciness, or even just one flavour that stands out amongst all others? Take plenty of time to savour the food, to hold it in your mouth and understand why you like it as much as you do.

8. Is it the *emotional association* with the food? Where does this come from? Does it remind you of family cooked dinners, with everyone sitting around the table? Or does it remind you of time alone, perhaps travelling abroad? Maybe it reminds you of a particular person or time in your life. Be aware of what emotional feelings are supporting the intense desire for the food.

9. Is it the *thoughts* in the mind? Is there a calming of thoughts as you relax into the food? Is there a feeling

of sanity as you focus intently on the taste and savour the flavours? How does the mind behave when you sit down to eat this food?

10. Or is it the *physical sensation* of eating the food? Is it that it leaves you feeling pleasantly heavy and sleepy, or perhaps excitable and active? Does it leave you feeling thin, toned and pleasantly full? Whatever it is, take the time to notice why you like the foods you like, and from where the desire to consume them comes. And, when you look at them in this way, take the time to notice whether you still feel the same amount of emotional attachment towards them.

Exercise 2: *Foods You Dislike*

1. Take a food that you really dislike and sit down at a table with it.
2. What's the first thing that comes into your mind when you look at it? What is it that fills you with dread? No matter what it is, continue to examine each of the following points, keeping in mind what it was that first came to mind.
3. Is it the way it *looks*? And if it is, what is it about the way it looks that disgusts you? Is it the colour, the shape, the resemblance to something else? Pick it up and look at it for what it is, rather than for what you think it is.
4. Is it the *smell* of the food? If it is, what is about the smell that you dislike so much? Is it the bitterness, the way it catches at the back of your throat, the way it

hangs in the air afterwards? Again, pick it up, smell it and try to understand what it is about the smell that you dislike.

5. Is it the *texture* of the food? If it is, what is it about the texture that puts you off? Is it the rough surface, smooth surface, the touch in your hand or the sensation in your mouth? Or is it simply the memory of a sensation, of how it felt before when you've eaten it?

6. Is it the *sound* of the food? If it is, what is about the sound that you dislike? Is it the abrasive noise it makes against a knife, the squeaky sound it creates when you chew, or the slurping sound as you suck it?

7. Is it the *taste* of the food? If it is the taste, then what is it about the taste that makes you shiver? Is it the sickly sweet taste, the bitterness, the saltiness or the spiciness? No matter how much you dislike the food, try putting it in your mouth and investigating the flavours. What's the worst that can happen?

8. Is it the *emotional association* with the food? Where does this come from? Does it take you back to difficult situations with family or friends? Does it remind you of a particular time in your life which you either disliked or now desperately want back? Notice the emotional feelings that arise when you try eating the food.

9. Is it the *thoughts* in the mind? Does the mind suddenly become very busy, does it cause lots of restlessness and agitation? Or does it leave you feeling guilty, frustrated or depressed? In short, how does the mind behave when you sit down to eat this food?

10. Or is it the *physical sensation* and after-effects of eating the food? Is it that it leaves you feeling sluggish, perhaps anxious with butterflies, or wired with shaky hands? Does it leave you feeling fat, bloated or out of shape? Whatever it is, take the time to notice why you dislike the foods you dislike, and from where the resistance comes. And with this new perspective, do you still feel the same amount of aversion and emotional discomfort towards that food?

So, how was it? Have you discovered anything new about your eating habits in trying either of these exercises? It's really important to remember that a mindful attitude is one of openness, honesty, curiosity and investigation. If we apply this attitude to our eating habits, then not only will we make discoveries about why we eat the way we do, but we will fundamentally transform the way we eat, perhaps even changing the foods we eat in the process. So often we project the 'idea' of something on to the experience of eating, rather than simply experiencing the moment for what it is. When we give up that tendency, then – and only then – changes begin. So, be bold in your food choices and commit to a more open and adventurous relationship with food if you can.

CHAPTER SEVEN

THE HEADSPACE 'TAKE10'
MINDFULNESS TECHNIQUE

INTRODUCTION

I cannot over-emphasise the importance of this chapter. Because no matter whether the research has focused on weight loss, self-esteem, heart disease, cholesterol levels or blood pressure, *every* clinical trial involving mindfulness has a regular, daily mindfulness practice at its core. In fact in many of the trials this is the *only* component. Participants are usually encouraged to build up the amount of time they dedicate to the exercise each day, and then to apply the idea throughout their daily lives. But the starting point is nearly always a short, manageable period of time, just like the one outlined in this chapter.

Despite such positive results published in respected medical journals all over the world, for many people it remains a complete mystery how focusing on the mind can have such a profound effect on the human body. But the science is there for anyone to see. And the more you practise this exercise, the more obvious the link between mind and body will become to you.

Like any skill, learning to be present requires practice. It's *possible* to learn mindfulness whilst walking down the road, chatting with friends, eating a meal, or even whilst hurtling towards the ground with a parachute on your back, but it's so much easier to learn whilst sitting still, free from distractions. Every skill in life requires a certain amount of focus, especially when you're learning how to do it, and the results will always be better when you give that skill your whole-hearted attention. Mindfulness is no exception. That's why this simple and easy-to-learn Take10 technique gets an entire chapter to itself.

Even though there's very little mention of food in this chapter, don't be tempted to skip over it. Not only would you be jeopardising the results of your 10-Day or, hopefully, your *lifelong* plan towards a new way of eating, but you would also be going against every bit of scientific research that has been carried out on mindfulness. Done on a regular basis, this type of exercise has been shown to have profound implications for physical, emotional and mental health. It is an exercise you can come back to each day, a safe place, where you can be sure of getting some headspace and perspective. It is an exercise that you can carry with you, wherever you go, which will only reinforce your application of mindfulness. Most importantly, it will help to give you the stability of awareness and emotion necessary to get in shape and stay in shape, for good.

A useful way of looking at Take10 is to view it as a magnifying glass for your mind. Scary thought, I know, but also very useful if you need to understand what's going on up there. Most of the time we're so preoccupied with doing things, or thinking about things, that we don't really have any idea what's going on in the present moment. It's as if we are so close to it, so caught up in it, that we can't really appreciate it or understand it for what it is. When we momentarily pause to watch the mind with a little more perspective, we begin to see all the thoughts and feelings in much more detail, as they appear in the present moment. For many people this is a revolutionary experience. No longer do they feel overwhelmed with thoughts (about food, their body or otherwise), but also they are no longer swept away by feelings of desire, anxiety, guilt or any other conflicting emotion. With Take10 you get the opportunity to step back and appreciate the big picture.

Now the interesting thing is, even if the thoughts and feelings do not revolve around your eating habits, esteem or body image, they are still every bit as relevant to understanding those things. Because, as much as we might like to separate and compartmentalise every single aspect of our life, ultimately life is just one, and so is the mind. An anxious mind is an anxious mind. The more you experience it around food, or in relation to your body image, the more it will be expressed and experienced in other areas of your life too – be that in your relationships, friendships, work life or social life. And the same is true for a busy mind, a restless mind, a guilty, sad, or addictive mind. We cannot experience these emotions in complete isolation. And as long as we want to keep these emotions at bay, there will always be tension or conflict in the mind. Because even when they are not present, there will be an underlying fear that they might suddenly arise. At first this can sound a bit abstract, but after several weeks of practising mindfulness it begins to make a lot more sense.

Take10 is an opportunity to see your mind in all its glory. It's an opportunity to see the thought patterns that govern your eating, to understand the emotions that influence your relationship with body image, and through that realisation to discover a sense of ease and underlying contentment that very few people ever get to experience. Oh, and just so you know, the science around mindfulness has also shown that when you do this on a regular basis, you are quite likely to experience considerable improvements in overall feelings of happiness and wellbeing too, but hopefully that won't put you off too much!

Before getting started with the exercise, there's one more bit of useful information I'd like to share with you. You'll get the most out of this technique if you think about it in quite a broad context. Traditionally it was taught in three parts. Now, although I'm not big on tradition for tradition's sake, I've always found that people get much more from this exercise when they stick to this tried-and-tested formula. So here are just a few words on the three parts of the exercise: approach, practice and integration.

APPROACH

How you approach the technique, and how you choose to relate to the contents of your mind, will define your experience of mindfulness and the resulting headspace. Get it right and your practice will fly; get it wrong and it could feel like a real struggle. It's difficult not to expect perfect results the first time around – that's just how we seem to be programmed these days. But the reality is that this exercise takes a little practice, like learning any other new kind of skill. So try to get used to the idea that your mind isn't going to stop whirring away just because you want it to, and that's really not the objective of the exercise anyway. The idea behind this technique is to discover a new way of relating to your thoughts and emotions, a way in which you can feel calmer, clearer and happier as a result – a way in which you can begin to make fundamental changes to the way you eat and the way you relate to your body. So, forget about any ideas of trying to clear the mind or stop your thoughts.

Aside from unrealistic expectations, the other big obstacle for most people is trying too hard. For some reason, most of us have been programmed with the idea that the harder we try, the better the results. But this is different. Discovering the calm and the clarity that you're looking for is less about 'doing' and more about 'not doing'. So take comfort in the fact that this is the one area of your life where you don't have to apply lots of effort to achieve your desired results. In fact, applying lots of effort can even be counter-productive. Imagine that, just sitting back and watching the mind without needing to do anything much at all – doesn't that sound inviting?

Whilst everything you need to find that kind of headspace can be found in this book, you might also like to visit www.headspace.com or download our app. You'll find some brilliant animations that will really help to clarify your under-standing. They might also make you smile. For those of you without access to the Internet, or who find the idea of technology off-putting, here's a taste of what you'll find in each of those animations.

Mind

Have you ever tried throwing a stone into a very still, clear pool of water? If you have, then you'll have noticed that as soon as the stone hits the water, it creates ripples on the surface. The more stones you throw in, the more ripples you get. And if you *keep* throwing stones, eventually the surface of the water becomes so clouded that you not only lose the sense of stillness, but you also lose the clarity, the ability to see into the water. The mind is quite similar to this in many ways, with every new thought having the potential to create this feeling of disturbance, or agitation, in both body and mind. It doesn't have to be that way, but that's normally how it feels for most people before they learn to do Take10.

But as you begin to sit on a daily basis and get used to just stepping back from it all, those ripples usually begin to calm down. And when that happens, you begin to get a bit more clarity. You get to actually look into the pool of water to see what's in there. It might not be what you want to see, or what you expect to see, but you need to be able to see these things in order to let go of them, and when you let go of them, life feels a little lighter. This is the dynamic of stillness and clarity that you'll discover when you sit down to Take10 each day.

Expectation

Another dynamic at play during Take10 is the movement of thought and the temptation to try and control everything. Imagine for a moment that you're sitting down at the edge of a very busy road. Now before you learn Take10, or any other mindfulness-based exercise, I think it's a bit like sitting on that grass verge with a blindfold on. Sure, you're aware of all the background noise, the movement of the cars, but you're not able to actually see clearly what it is that's causing the disturbance. Now when you sit to get some headspace, it's a bit like taking the blindfold off: all of a sudden you see much more clearly the thoughts and feelings in the mind. You get to understand how and why you feel the way you do.

The temptation is often to run out into the road and start trying to control the traffic. This involves chasing after the pleasant thoughts (the nice-looking cars), and trying to stop all the unpleasant thoughts (the dirty big lorries). But that's an exhausting way to live and not a very skilful way of dealing with the mind. So, Take1o requires a slightly different approach. It's about 'holding your seat' on the side of the road, and becoming comfortable with that autonomous flow of traffic, allowing it to come and go. And the funny thing is, when you do this, when you give up trying to control the mind as we usually do, what you'll generally find is that the volume of traffic on the road starts to *decrease*, and the space between the cars starts to *increase*. And that's the place of calm and clarity that feels so nice. So you can see that the approach to getting some headspace is *less* about control and *more* about perspective.

Effort

As I said before, when you learn a new exercise, the temptation is to apply a lot of effort, to concentrate very hard, the idea being that the more effort you apply, the quicker the results, or perhaps the *better* the results. But getting some headspace with Take1o is a little bit different from that. In fact, I think it's a bit like sleep in that way. I don't know if you've ever experienced that feeling of lying in bed and not being able to go to sleep, but the more you try to go to sleep, the further you move away from it. You can't force sleep, right? It's exactly the same with getting some headspace. You can't *force* headspace; you can't *force* a state of relaxation and calm. It's something that happens very naturally, gradually, on its own terms.

One of the best metaphors I've heard for this process is that of taming a wild horse. If you look at how a wild horse is tamed, rather than pinning it down in one place, the horse is led out on a very long rope, and put in a big, open, spacious field. The horse runs round feeling as if it's got all the space in the world and then very slowly the rope is brought in. The horse adjusts to this feeling quite easily, until it comes to a natural place of rest. And we're looking to do just the same thing with the mind in Take10. It's not about pinning the mind down and concentrating with laser-like focus. Instead, it's about giving the mind lots of space and, using the prescribed technique, allowing it to come to a natural place of rest.

Blue Sky

This particular metaphor is quite possibly my favourite, and if you can remember this when you go to do Take10 each day, then you really can't go too far wrong. So, take a moment to think how it feels when you imagine a very clear blue sky. My guess is it feels pretty nice. OK, so what about when you imagine a very dark, stormy, cloudy sky? For most people, that probably won't feel quite as nice. But the thing is, even on a very cloudy day, the blue sky is still there. If you get on a plane and fly up through the clouds, the sky's still blue. It's just that we forget; we get so fixated on the clouds that we forget that the sky is still blue on the other side.

This is such a good analogy for the mind. It can be so tempting to sit there *trying* to relax, *trying* to gain a sense of calm, clarity or headspace. But *trying* is really the antithesis of relaxation, so it's no surprise that this approach doesn't usually work so well. So, rather than trying to create a state of blue sky, a state of happiness and calm, it's more a question of setting up a deck-chair in the back garden, sitting back, and waiting for the clouds to pass.

PRACTICE

The practice is the bit when you actually apply the instructions, sitting down to do the technique without any distractions. You'll be applying mindfulness to your eating and maybe other areas of your life too, but this is the part when you can really get familiar with what it means to be in the here and now, making it that much easier to apply to every other moment of the day. The technique is explained below, but you may prefer to go online at www.headspace.com, where I'll talk you through the different steps. If you don't fancy the idea of sitting at your computer to do the exercise, then you can also download the Headspace app, which will mean you can listen to it anywhere, and even take it on holiday with you. In case you're wondering, Take10 is entirely free to access online or within the app, but you might prefer to follow the instructions below, which will explain in detail everything you need to know.

TAKE 10

Having understood how best to approach the exercise, as well as the potential for how it can be integrated into everyday life, it's now time to have a look at the practice component – the exercise itself. I've split it into 10 easy-to-follow steps. If you're learning it directly from this book, then you may find that it takes you a few days to remember all the different steps, and if you find yourself having to open your eyes halfway through to check where you're up to, that's absolutely fine. But do remember that you can listen to a guided version completely free of charge.

Step 1: Get Settled . . .

Find a quiet space where you can relax.

Sit comfortably in a chair with your hands resting in your lap or on your knees. Try to keep your back straight, but without forcing it. Sitting at the front of the chair can often help. Your neck should be relaxed, with your chin just slightly tucked in.

Whether you're using your own timer, or following one of the Headspace guided techniques, commit to practising for the full time you've set aside (10 minutes to begin with), regardless of whether that feels easy or difficult.

Step 2: Breathe Deeply . . .

Defocus your eyes, gazing softly into the middle distance.

Take five deep, audible breaths, breathing in through the nose and out through the mouth. As you breathe in, focus on the chest expanding and your lungs filling with air. As you breathe out, focus on the body exhaling and letting go of any physical tension.

On the last exhalation, gently close your eyes and allow the breath to return to its natural rhythm, in and out of the nose.

Step 3: Check-in . . .

Take a few moments to settle into your body. Observe your posture, noticing the sensations where your body presses against the chair and where your feet meet the ground. You can also notice the weight of your arms and hands resting on your legs.

Acknowledge your other senses too – notice anything you can smell, hear or taste, any sensations of heat or cold. Take a good minute or so to do this.

The more genuinely interested or curious you are about noticing these things, the more your meditation will benefit from this part of the process.

Step 4: Scan Your Body . . .

Slowly turn your mind inwards and begin to scan your whole body from head to toe. Notice which areas feel uncomfortable or tense, and which areas feel relaxed and at ease. Take a good 30 seconds to do the scan, really taking time to build up an accurate picture of how the body is feeling. You might even like to repeat it several times.

If you can, avoid the temptation to try and change any unpleasant feelings by shifting posture, instead simply acknowledging the discomfort and continuing with the scan. Don't forget to notice the smaller parts of the body, like the fingers and toes, and even your ears.

As you become more aware of the physical sensations, you might also become more aware of your underlying mood – the emotional quality of the mind. As much as possible, try to be aware of this without judging it or getting into any kind of analysis. And if there's nothing very obvious there, don't worry, that's fine too.

Step 5: Consider the 'Why' . . .

Pause for around 30 seconds to consider why you're sitting to meditate. This might sound obvious, but it's surprisingly easy to do something without being clear as to your true motivation. For example, you might realise you're planning to try and stop all your thoughts or get rid of uncomfortable feelings. So remind yourself of the approach again and be clear that Take10 is not about trying to control the mind.

Next, take a moment to consider the wider effects of doing this exercise each day. Sure, feeling calmer and less stressed will help 'you' to feel better, will help 'you' to make better choices, but that has a knock-on effect for the people around you too – from family and friends, to your colleagues at work, and, who knows, maybe even the bus driver. I suppose you could call it a 'ripple effect'.

Step 6: One Last Reminder . . .

Before you start to focus on the breath, always remind yourself that getting some headspace is less about 'doing' and more about 'not doing'. OK, so I'm going to ask you to watch the breath for a short time, but the body takes care of the breathing, which means all you need to do is to watch it. Your only job is to step back and allow the body and mind to unwind – in their own way, and in their own time.

Reflecting on that idea of blue sky from the approach section will help strengthen this idea. If you can watch the animation on the website before you begin, that will help to reinforce it.

Step 7: Observe the Breath . . .

Bring your attention to the breath. Don't make any effort to change it in any way, just observe the rising and falling sensation that it creates in the body. Notice where these sensations occur – be it in the belly, chest, shoulders, or anywhere else in the body for that matter.

And whilst you're watching this movement, start to notice the quality of each breath – whether it's deep or shallow, long or short, fast or slow, regular or irregular. Again, there's no need to try and change it; instead just be aware of the sensation.

Having got a feel for this, begin silently counting each time you inhale or exhale – this will make it easier to maintain your focus. So, count 1 as you follow the inhalation, 2 as you follow the exhalation, then 3 on the next inhalation, and so on up to a count of 10. Then start again at 1.

It's completely normal for thoughts to bubble up whilst you're doing this, so don't worry if the mind wanders off every now and again. But as soon as you realise you've got caught up in thought, gently guide your attention back to the breath. If you can remember the number you'd counted up to, then pick it up from there – alternatively you can just start again at 1.

Continue watching the breath in this way until the timer sounds or, if you're listening to the audio track, I guide you on to the next step.

Step 8: Allow Your Mind to be Free . . .

Now let go of any focus at all – you don't even need to focus on the breath any more. You might find yourself inundated with thoughts and plans, or feel totally calm and relaxed. At this particular stage it really doesn't matter too much. Allow your mind to be free in this way for about 20 or 30 seconds.

Whatever happens at this stage is absolutely fine and there's no particular result or effect you should be looking for. So, with that in mind, and no sense of effort or control, simply enjoy the rare opportunity to let your mind be exactly as it is.

Step 9: Prepare to Finish . . .

Become aware once more of the other physical sensations – of the body on the chair, your feet on the floor, and of the weight of the arms and hands resting in your lap. You might also like to notice any sounds, smells, tastes or other sensations which will help to bring you back into your immediate surroundings.

When you're ready, slowly open your eyes, finishing as you began – sitting upright in the chair, eyes open but with a soft focus. Maintain that position for 10 seconds or so, appreciating the moment. You can then sit back and have a stretch.

Step 10: Take it With You . . .

Before standing up, form a clear idea about what you're going to do next. For example, are you going to the bathroom to brush your teeth, to the kitchen to make a cup of tea, or to pick up your keys before leaving the house? It's so easy to just jump up off the seat and lose the calm and spacious quality you've so carefully cultivated. So try to carry this awareness with you to the next activity.

And look for small moments throughout the day to remind yourself of what it feels like to have that clarity and focused attention. Maybe it's when you first sit down at your desk at work, when you drink your morning coffee, or when you're on the bus. You don't need to do the whole exercise, but just take a couple of deep breaths and then notice how you feel – physically, mentally and emotionally.

So, how did you get on? Don't worry if it didn't go quite as I describe it and you found yourself drifting off and remember to refer back to the approach section if you are unsure about how to set about doing the exercise. The most important thing is to do it regularly, daily if possible. That's how the mind will best become familiar with the technique. Despite the fact we're talking about less than 1 per cent of the day, it's surprising how many people find it difficult to take 10 minutes out on a regular basis. In fact, you may already be finding yourself thinking of reasons why you couldn't possibly fit it into your schedule. It's for this reason I've come up with these 10 tips to ensure that you make it happen, each and every day.

1. Just do it (but do it gently)

It may sound obvious, but this exercise will only work if you actually do it. It works even better if you do it on a regular basis . . . and even better than that if you follow this tried-and-tested approach. When it comes to getting some headspace, just a very small commitment can lead to very big changes. Sure, reading and talking about the mind can be inspiring, but the magic happens when you sit down and close your eyes.

2. One day at a time

Just like learning any other skill, this exercise requires practice. It's not about doing as much as possible, but rather regular, consistent practice, which will allow your brain to rewire itself. So, it's worth remembering that this is a skill for life, something which will continue to develop and evolve for as long as you continue to do it.

But it might feel a bit more manageable if you take it just one day at a time.

3. Making it happen

Do you ever forget to take a shower? My guess is, probably not (or you'd soon hear about it from your friends). The reason you don't forget is because it's part of your everyday routine – it's simply what you do. After a little while the same will be true of this exercise . . . you won't even need to think about it. So, find a place for this technique in the day, give it a home, and, if necessary, set a reminder in the diary.

4. Same time, same place

Part of establishing a healthy new habit is routine. If you sit to get some headspace just before breakfast each day (for example), then you're much more likely to remember to do it, and if you have the same familiar space to go back to each day as well, then that's a real bonus. Sure, you might need to be flexible sometimes, but as much as possible think 'same time, same place'.

5. Clean and tidy

Even though you may have your eyes closed most of the time, sitting in a messy room with lots of stuff all around you is probably not the most conducive environment to sit and get some headspace. Don't worry, it doesn't have to be spotless, and ultimately it's possible to do this exercise anywhere. But to begin with, a nice clear, clean and tidy space can really help to relax the mind before you begin your practice.

6. Tick-tock

Although the idea of setting a timer can be off-putting at first, it's important to remember why it's there. Rather than putting an 'emphasis' on time, the timer actually allows you to 'forget' about time. In this way it helps you to find that balance of relaxation and focus in your practice. But remember to choose a quiet, gentle alarm, otherwise it might feel like a rather abrupt end to the exercise. If you're using the guided meditation you won't need to worry about this, as I'll talk you through it in just the right time.

7. The finishing line

Sometimes you might enjoy the exercise so much that you'll be tempted to continue, even after the alarm has gone off. At other times, the mind might appear so busy that you want to give up after just two minutes. But the best way to train the mind is to simply sit until the timer goes off, always finishing the practice then, no matter how you feel – because that way you'll develop a very honest practice, with very real perspective.

8. Keep it light

Although it's important to have a serious commitment to the exercise (because that's the only way to experience the full range of benefits), it shouldn't feel so serious that it becomes a chore. After all, sitting down to take 10 minutes out each day is actually a real treat. It's your time to relax and unwind. It will only feel like a chore if you think there is something you need to achieve, so remember to keep it light.

9. Motivation is everything

A limited mind is a limited practice, so think big with this exercise. When you sit to do it, remember that it is not just for you, but also for all those around you – the people you interact with every day, and even the people they then interact with (a sort of ripple effect). If you remember to do this, then you'll find the exercise much easier. Not only that, but the exercise will have a much greater sense of meaning and importance for you.

10.Nothing to achieve

Remember the blue sky. No matter what you take from this book, remember the idea of the blue sky. When you sit to do this exercise, there is no 'thing' to achieve or create, because that 'thing' (the blue sky, aka underlying happiness) is already there. So you don't need to apply lots of effort in trying to make more of it, but instead step back and watch as the clouds begin to part . . . to reveal exactly what it is you've been looking for.

INTEGRATION

This final component of the exercise is where mindfulness starts to get really interesting. Because it's where you get the opportunity to integrate the calm and clarity you've developed during the practice section into your everyday life. This is especially relevant given the focus of this book on mindful eating. Remember, mindfulness means to be present, in the moment. And if you can do it sitting on a chair, then why not whilst out shopping, drinking a cup of tea, eating your food, holding the baby, working at the computer, or having a chat with a friend? All of these are opportunities to apply mindfulness, to be aware.

This means that rather than drifting through the day on autopilot, not really being fully conscious of the decisions you make, you move from one moment to the next with a sense of calm and clarity in the mind. It means that rather than daydreaming about doughnuts, or the new health regime you're about to start (always next Monday), you'll be in the here and now, experiencing life as it unfolds around you. As I said in the Introduction, researchers have found that most people are caught up in thought for between 30 per cent and 50 per cent of the time, even whilst engaged in activities. They also discovered this mind wandering was a direct cause of unhappiness and confusion. So, alongside your goals and ambitions for finding your ideal weight and getting some headspace around food and your body, this is just one more reason to integrate mindfulness into your life.

This book is full of examples of how to apply mindfulness to your eating habits, but why limit it to food-related activities? Here are five other situations to which you could easily apply mindfulness on a daily basis, and yet during which typically the mind is wandering. Remember, the stronger your practice and the more familiar you are with mindfulness in everyday life, the easier you'll find it to apply to food and your body, and the more likely you are to reach your desired weight. As always, the same rules apply. It's not about trying to stop thoughts and feelings, but instead learning to step back from them, allowing them to come and go. And if you do find yourself suddenly lost in thought, then no problem at all, simply bring your attention back to the physical senses and whatever it is you're doing.

1. Brushing your teeth

Old way: Vague awareness of picking up your tooth-brush and moving it around the mouth on autopilot, as you wander around the house, tripping over the cat, looking for your keys, mentally preparing for your first meeting of the day, whilst wondering who'll play James Bond after Daniel Craig.

New way: Being mindful of the feet on the floor, the temperature and the texture on the soles of your feet; mindful of the appearance, smell, flavour and texture of the toothpaste; mindful of the arm moving from side to side and the sound of the brush against your teeth; mindful of each and every tooth and the sensation of the brush against the gums.

Not only will you feel calm and collected afterwards, but your dentist will be happy with you too – you might even get a sugar-free lollipop!

2. Having a shower

Old way: Acute awareness of scolding hot water alternating with freezing cold water until you find the sweet spot. From then on in, the mind wanders off to the eternal question of 'What *would* it be like to win *The X Factor*?' as you sing your favourite tune into the shower head.

New way: Being mindful of the need to set the tempera-ture *before* getting into the shower; mindful of the wave of pleasure as the warm water washes over you; mindful of the smell of the shower gel, soap or shampoo; mindful of the mind jumping forwards, imagining conversations that have yet to happen; mindful of the amount of water you're using; and mindful of the sound of the water coming to a stop.

Greenpeace will love you for it, and you'll end up with a much clearer mind for the day ahead.

3. Commuting to work

Old way: Standing like a sardine squashed into a tin can on a train or bus, resenting anyone who has a seat, feeling nauseous at the potent cocktail of perfumes, aftershaves, deodorants and hairsprays, whilst trying to keep your cool as a pram rocks back and forth into your shins. Alternatively, sitting in the relative comfort of a car, but in traffic so slow that you fear you might actually have to put the car into reverse.

New way: Being mindful of your environment and the tendency to resist it; being mindful of the emotions as they rise and fall, come and go; mindful of all the different senses, but rather than thinking about them, judging them, or analysing them, simply acknowledging them; mindful of wanting to be somewhere else, of wishing time away; and mindful of wanting to scream out loud or put your foot down in the car.

The other people around you will almost certainly appreciate your lack of road-rage, train-rage or bus-rage and, you never know, you may even find yourself turning up to work with a smile on your face.

4. Washing the dishes

Old way: Vaguely aware of the need to avoid the sharp knife, hidden beneath the plates in the water, as you stare out of the window and wonder why Mrs green coat with the brown shoes from number 48 doesn't get together with Mr square jaw with the fancy car from number 32. I mean, they're both single, and they look as though they'd be perfect together.

New way: Being mindful of the very first moment when your hands meet the water; mindful of the warmth and the transference of heat to the body; mindful of picking up one thing at a time and taking just an extra second or two to clean it thoroughly; mindful of the passing thoughts and of letting them go; mindful of seeing people come and go through the window without getting involved in any storylines; mindful of wanting to get on and do something else; and mindful of feeling satisfied when you've finished.

OK, so you have a dishwasher, but you get the picture. And if the dishwasher ever breaks down, you'll know that it is possible to get some headspace whilst washing the dishes.

5. Standing in a queue

Old way: As you stand there tapping your foot, arms crossed and jaws clenched, you wonder why everyone else has chosen the exact same time as you to come to the bank. As you flick through old texts and emails on your mobile, desperately searching for something, anything, to do to escape your own impatience, you consider the possibility of robbing the place one day (hypothetically of course), absent-mindedly looking to see where the different cameras are and, thereby, getting your picture saved to yet another database in the sky.

New way: Being mindful of the sense of urgency with which you enter the bank; mindful of your reaction when you first see the queue; mindful of your posture as you stand there waiting; mindful of your breath as you focus on the physical sensations in the body; mindful of your reaction each time the queue creeps forward; mindful of the tendency to keep looking at your watch, checking your phone or looking for some kind of distraction; and mindful of your interaction with another human being when you finally get served.

You can see the queue as an irritating inconvenience, or as an opportunity to take a break. Either way, you know you're not *really* going to rob the bank, so why are you even looking?

CHAPTER EIGHT

MINDFUL EATING
(THE HEADSPACE WAY)

Having introduced you to Take10, it's now time to take a look at the practice of mindful eating itself. As I said earlier, the heart of this technique has been around for several thousand years. I've made a few adaptations to make it more relevant to your everyday experience in the modern world, but the fundamentals have been kept just as they always have been. I can't emphasise enough just how important this is, in terms of feeling confident and trusting a technique that has been tried and tested, developed and refined, used with so many people – successfully – in every type of culture, with every variety of diet, and over such a long time.

One of the main adaptations I've made is to add sections on shopping lists, shopping, the preparation of food and cooking into the equation, alongside the actual consumption of food. It's reasonable to assume that when mindful eating was first conceived of, there was not quite the same diversity of choice we have these days. Foraging in the forest isn't quite the same as checking out the frozen food aisle in the supermarket. In fact it was probably difficult to go too far wrong in terms of selecting healthy foods back then.

175

To really understand mindful eating in its widest context, it's important to incorporate a mindful approach to all of these aspects into your life: food selection, food shopping, food preparation, cooking and eating. This chapter explains the thinking behind each mindful aspect, before introducing a specific exercise for each one. Oh, and whilst eating may sound like the most important of the five aspects in helping you to achieve your goals, the other four areas will undoubtedly influence what you end up putting in your mouth. In case you're tempted to skip ahead to the techniques, it's worth remembering that preparation is everything. Just as with the Take10 technique, the way you approach the techniques will define the outcome. So, if you are really serious about changing, then it's most definitely worth taking an extra few minutes to understand the philosophy of mindful eating and how you can get the best from each and every part of the technique.

MINDFUL FOOD SELECTION

Are you the kind of person who will just eat whatever there is in the cupboard or fridge? If there's chocolate in the house or a packet of biscuits open, are you likely to finish them off? If you are a Nibbler, a Gorger, a Binger, a Zombie or a Comfort Eater, the answer will almost inevitably be 'yes'. In fact, even if you're from one of the other foodie groups, there's a pretty good chance you might indulge the temptation. If this is the case, consider for a moment how it might be if you didn't have these foods immediately to hand. Hardly rocket science, I know, but it's amazing how often we forget this simple fact. If we stock our cupboards with heavily processed, overly refined, unhealthy foods and snacks, then that is exactly what we are going to end up eating. Sure, if you don't have those foods available you might still feel the urge to have an unhealthy snack, but it will require a lot more effort (and bravery) to go out in your dressing gown at 11 p.m. to buy something. Needless to say, for most people, that will probably be the difference between eating it and not eating it.

Have you ever stopped to think why you buy the foods you buy? Could it be that you get them simply because you always have? Not so long ago a well-known food company did some research into the different types of sandwiches on sale. Whilst new varieties of sandwiches in the UK were performing well, the old staples of prawn mayo, ham and cheese, chicken and salad and so on consistently outsold anything new. They found that many people, on a daily basis, would browse all the different types on offer before choosing the same one that they always chose. Sound familiar?

When it comes to food (and most things in life for that matter), we truly are creatures of habit. We go for what we know, what we are used to. A long time ago this made sense and ensured we were eating foods that were safe, foods that wouldn't do us any harm. But times have changed. There is now such an enormous variety of food available that we don't need to be restricted by the often calorie-dense food choices of our youth. As comforting as it might be to have eggs and bacon for breakfast every morning, or sticky toffee pudding for dinner every night, they are not going to help you to reach your ideal weight. But you already know that.

Take a moment to think why you bought the foods you did

last time you went shopping. Was it out of habit – you used to eat it as a child, or buy it as a student and have just bought it ever since? Was it because the food was on special offer – perhaps a 2-for-1 deal? Was it because of how it looked, the way it was packaged and marketed? Was it because it was quick and easy to prepare – a microwave meal or ready-prepared salad? Was it because you were feeling down and thought you deserved a treat to pick you back up? Or was it because you'd heard that it was healthy, that it might help you to lose weight? Perhaps it was an advert you'd seen – stuck conveniently between your favourite TV programmes – urging you to buy more of them. Or maybe it was because your friend is always eating it – and they're in great shape so it must be good for you too. Sure, you *might* have bought it simply because you enjoy it, but funnily enough that is rarely our sole motivation for selecting the foods that we do.

You may well find that this process alone will help you sift out some of the foods that are not particularly conducive to getting to a place of ease and comfort with your body and diet. It can sometimes feel a bit like waking up from a dream, when you look at the food and think, 'Why did I even buy that?' Just as importantly, though, it is also about recognising those foods that you associate with being healthy, buy religiously, and yet dislike with a passion. Holding your nose to get food down your throat, or stockpiling enough seeds and nuts to feed every passing migrating bird is no way to live life, and is completely unnecessary if you follow *The Headspace Diet*.

The starting point for making a mindful shopping list is to be in a good place mentally when you write it down; to have a sense of calm on the one hand and clarity on the other. The next thing is to ask yourself: 'What does my body need to function at its optimum level?' And why would you want anything less than that? Why would you not want to feel your best, to look your best, to be at ease with how you look, and have peace of mind with what you are putting into your body? Surely, to do anything else would be madness, right? So, this is our starting point for making the list.

If you are struggling for ideas for what to put on your list, then you might like to check out Chapter 10, *The Headspace Diet* Handy Nutrition Guide. Put together with the help and assistance of our in-house Exercise Physiologist and Dietary Consultant, it will give you lots of useful information on where to get started.

The next thing to consider is how your food selection matches up with the other four aspects of mindful eating. Do your food choices mean that you will have to spend half the week trekking around the shops trying to find obscure items? Fine if it does, and if you're a Gourmet or Eco-Geek you'll probably be used to it already, but be realistic as to how much time you're willing to invest in finding what you want. Also, take a moment to consider how likely it is that you will have the time and inclination to prepare these foods. Whilst this may be no problem for the Bear or the Calorie Counter, if you currently eat like a Gorger, then moving from high-speed, fast-food, microwave-ready meals to vegetable casseroles will take a little bit of adjustment. Likewise, it's all very well buying tins of chickpeas to eat, but if they sit collecting dust in the cupboard because you're not sure how to cook them and have no wish to learn, then there is little point in buying them.

So, make sure that the foods you choose to put on your

shopping list are foods that you enjoy, and buy them in appropriate quantities. It sounds obvious, but so much food is wasted either because we buy foods that we think we 'should' eat and then don't eat them, or because we overestimate how much we need and then have to throw food away. This is such an important point. In order to have a good relationship with food we need to enjoy its company. If we resist the things we like too strongly, we will simply build up a feeling of resentment at not being allowed the freedom to enjoy them. So it is about having a balance between what we know is good for us, and what we genuinely enjoy. Often it is simply a case of trying new foods and expanding your diet, so that old and unhealthy favourites can be replaced with new-to-you, healthier options.

HEADSPACE MINDFUL FOOD SELECTION: EXERCISE

Next time you have a bit of free time at home, empty a cupboard of food, one thing at a time, or alternatively do a few shelves in the fridge. Make sure you've got enough room to separate the foods into different piles. You might find it more comfortable to sit down to do this, but you can also do it standing. Like most of the exercises in this book, you'll get the most out of this exercise if you turn off your mobile and limit any other distractions or noise.

1. Begin by gently closing your eyes and taking a few
   deep breaths. Leave behind whatever you've been
   doing, knowing that you can return to it when you've

finished the exercise. Try and focus on the lungs filling with air as you breathe in through the nose, the mind settling and the body softening as you exhale through the mouth. When you've done this four or five times, you can gently open your eyes again and allow your breathing to return to its natural rhythm.

2. Next, pick up an item and see how it makes you feel. Does it make you feel happy, excited, anxious, bored, depressed, angry, guilty, or any other particularly strong emotion? Without trying to change the emotion, simply acknowledge it for what it is.

3. Notice whether you feel a strong sense of desire or resistance towards the food, or does it leave you feeling neither one way or the other? Try not to rush this process if possible – take a good 10 seconds or so before deciding exactly how it makes you feel.

4. If it's a pleasant feeling that arises, then take a moment or two to sit with that feeling, before moving on to the next step. Notice how both the body and mind experience this feeling. Is it a physical sensation, a memory, an idea, or a combination of them all?

5. If it's an unpleasant or difficult emotion that arises, take a little longer to sit with it. Without trying to escape the feeling or distract yourself from it in any way whatsoever, just allow it to be present, giving it the space that it needs to breathe.

6. Regardless of how it made you feel, try to be aware of your reaction to that emotion. Because funnily enough it is often the *reaction* to an emotion that causes the tension and confusion in the mind, rather than the initial emotion. For example, hating feelings of desire and wishing to be rid of them can often increase their frequency and make them even stronger. There's no need to analyse: simply notice and acknowledge.

7. Next, take a moment to consider why you bought the food in the first place. It's not enough to say 'because I always do' or 'because we need it', as there are choices to be found in everything. So, in the interests of achieving your ideal weight, be clear in your own mind as to what your primary motivation was. Choosing from the following list can often make it easier. You can even label a few Post-it notes and stick them on the table to create 10 different piles of food.

- Value (financial reasons)
- Taste (sensory pleasure)
- Spontaneity (emotional triggers)
- Habit (repetitive buying)
- Security (comfort foods)
- Health (internal wellbeing)
- Diet (aesthetic wellbeing)
- Ease (quick preparation)
- Appearance (fancy packaging)
- Status (social kudos)

8. Having finished the exercise for the chosen cupboard or fridge shelf (or both), take a moment to see what changes you might like to make. Remember, motivation is everything. If your intention is to give your body what it needs to operate at its optimum level, and to find its natural, most comfortable weight, then it is essential to give it the foods that will enable that process to happen.

9. Resolve to change any shopping habits you find unhelpful, uncomfortable or destructive, and only buy foods that will help to encourage a sense of *ease* in the mind, and a sense of *comfort* in the body. It is only when the natural intelligence of both body and mind come together that you will find your ideal weight, shape and size.

10. Finally, make out your new shopping list, being mindful of what you've just discovered about yourself and your shopping habits, mindful of the choices you've made in the past and your reasons for making them, and mindful of how you now intend to shop in the future.

MINDFUL FOOD SHOPPING

If you have a bit of free time, it's worth going into a supermarket simply to notice the carefully designed layouts (trying not to look like a shoplifter in the process). The first thing you'll probably notice is that everything is screaming for your attention.

Billions of pounds go into creating the perfect packaging, the colours, textures and materials that are used to present these foods in the most appealing way. Likewise, food positioning and product placement is a science of its own. The one and only purpose of this science is to make sure that we buy the products they want to sell us, regardless of our own aims and ambitions for a healthy diet and a mindful relationship with food.

For example, did you know that supermarkets will place items they are keen to push at precisely 20–30 degrees below eye-level, which is where most people will naturally hold their gaze whilst shopping? Have you ever noticed how the mainstream items you actually *need* are tucked away in the very far corner of the shop, meaning you have to go past all the other tempting foods in order to get to them? And what about food at the end of the aisles, conveniently placed for maximum attention and where you will, apparently, be 30 per cent more likely to pick up the food and put it in your trolley? And let's not even begin with the special offers. Most people I know have taken up so many three-for-two offers that they have enough tins in the cupboard to survive a nuclear war.

It doesn't just stop with what we can see with our eyes either. It's well known that supermarkets often divert the flow of air from the in-store bakery to the front entrance, so that the very first thing we smell when we walk in the shop is freshly baked bread and biscuits. If there is one smell that is going to get the salivary glands going, our digestive fluids excited, and get us filling up our baskets and trolleys with spontaneous purchases that we had no intention of buying, then that would be it. And then of course there are the little taster stations that pop up around the store. So, just in case we can't *see* it or *smell* it, there is the opportunity to *taste* it and make yet another on-the-spot purchase. Don't get me wrong, I'm a big fan of spontaneity; however, in this particular context, and in the interests of reaching your ideal shape and size, you may well find it easier if you shop with a very clear idea of what you intend to purchase.

When we go into these places with a busy mind, or when we're unclear about what we are going to buy or, worst of all, when we're feeling really hungry, we tend to make bad choices. Then once we get home and realise we've made those choices, we've usually already resigned ourselves to the fact that we're just going to have to eat them all anyway, starting that pesky diet next Monday instead. How many times have you wandered into a shop, seen something on the shelf that you had no intention of buying, and then without another thought just picked it up and put it in your basket? This is undoubtedly Zombie territory and it's surprising how often it happens. And all because, for that particular moment in time, we are mindless, distracted, caught up in thoughts or swept away by feelings. It's not wrong, but neither is it particularly helpful. Mindfulness shows you how to get those moments back.

Many people I've met say they just can't help themselves, that things happen so quickly, that the decision has been made before they are even aware of it. But if we all did every little thing that popped into our mind without thinking about the consequences, there would be complete chaos in the world (even more than there is already). So clearly the mechanism we are looking for is actually already in place. Because the truth is, we all have a filter that stops us doing things that are harmful, hurtful, dangerous or socially unacceptable. It just depends what we choose to point that filter towards and what level we choose to set it at.

Think about it, have you ever seen someone in the street that you fancy so much that you just want to walk right up to them and give them a kiss? But do you do it? I'm guessing probably not. Likewise, have you ever had a dangerous driver swerve in front of you (or into you) for no apparent reason? Was the initial thought to get them back in some way or to let them know that you're annoyed? But did you chase after them and give them a mouthful? Again, I'm assuming not. These thoughts and instinctive emotions are completely normal and there is nothing to feel uncomfortable about experiencing them. However, it is useful to notice that in these situations we don't usually follow through with the thought or the feeling simply because it arose in the mind. For whatever reason, whether it's because we think it is too dangerous, unwise, unsightly or immoral, we make the conscious choice not to go through with it. But when it comes to buying food, it is so much more difficult to see the consequences, and so it is that much easier to simply indulge the thought. But what if we started to bring the same clarity and gentle restraint to our food shopping habits that we employ in other areas of our life?

Mindful shopping is not just about the foods that you *buy* though. In fact it's potentially as broad as you choose to make it and there is a strong degree of overlap with the mindful selection of food in many places. For some people, mindful shopping will incorporate ethical questions as to where the food has been sourced, whether it promotes sustainable production of the food, appropriate and fair rewards for those involved in that production, and about the environmental impact of transporting the food to the shop. It may take into account deeply held beliefs based on a particular faith or path in life, and possibly the pros and cons of eating a vegetarian diet. It may raise questions about the use of chemicals and pesticides, or genetically modified materials. For others, it might raise issues regarding the changing landscape of the high street and the increasing monopoly of supermarkets, or the desire to support the community by buying local, seasonal produce, and so on.

These are all important questions and you will have your own unique relationship with each of them, especially if you veer towards the Eco-Geek way of eating. Some of these topics may appear important, whilst others you'll find difficult to relate to. Whatever your position, that's quite OK and it will in no way detract from the benefits of eating mindfully. But you may well find that when you start to shop mindfully, over time some of these issues become more important for you, and may even influence your food choices. So while mindful eating will help you reach your ideal shape and size, it will at the same time encourage a strong sense of responsibility. It doesn't try to, and nowhere in this book do I focus on that at any length. It just happens to be a natural consequence of becoming ever more mindful of living in the here and now. This in turn brings a greater understanding of just how interdependent we all are, and can help us to see our place in the world more clearly.

I've referred almost exclusively to supermarket shopping in this chapter (and indeed throughout the book), primarily because supermarkets control over 80 per cent of the grocery market in the UK. Needless to say, there are many wonderful smaller shops out there that I would actively encourage you to use and support whenever possible. Of course, there are time constraints, financial pressures, parking restrictions and a hundred and one other reasons for not visiting those shops, but there are plenty of reasons to *start* shopping there too. In fact, you may well find that as some of these questions become more important to you, many of these smaller shops offering ethically sourced, sustainably packaged (or even unpackaged) goods will quench your new-found desire for responsible shopping.

HEADSPACE MINDFUL FOOD SHOPPING: EXERCISE 1

This first exercise is for when you have some free time and are feeling genuinely curious as to why you continue to buy the foods that you do, even the ones you no longer want to. It's best if you're not in a hurry and you may find it more interesting, and possibly more fun, to do it with another person. Whatever you decide, make sure you are not in the shop to buy anything, and notice how the mind may well try and persuade you otherwise whilst there. Also, make sure you've eaten beforehand, as any feelings of hunger will almost certainly influence your thinking.

1. Begin by walking into the shop and noticing the very first thing that comes into your awareness. Is it the eyes that are first engaged, or perhaps the nose? If it's a very busy shop it may even be the ears. Take a moment to see what sense is most active for you at that particular time.

2. Without getting in anyone else's way, stand to one side and take a moment to notice whether there is a positive

or negative association with entering the food shop and with those first moments of awareness. Does it make you feel comfortable or uncomfortable?

3. Next, try to identify *exactly* how it makes you feel, both physically and mentally. Does it make you feel excited, anxious, happy, or does it make you feel bored, sluggish and lazy? Does it feel overwhelming in any way? You don't have to do anything about the feeling, simply noticing what it is and acknowledging it is quite enough for now.

4. As you begin to walk around the shop, take a good look at the placement of the foods. Which ones are up high, which ones are down low, and which ones have been placed right at eye-level, making them almost impossible to miss? Food companies pay supermarkets a lot of money to get their foods displayed in the right place, but how many of those at eye-level would you consider healthy?

5. Now search out one of your favourite snacks, preferably something you'd consider a 'guilty pleasure'. How does it feel when you see it on the shelf? Do you find yourself experiencing a surge of desire? As you've already resolved not to buy anything on this visit, this is a really unique opportunity to step back and look at the food in a wholly different and more objective way. How does the body feel in this moment?

6. So, what is it that makes the food seem so irresistible? Is it the packaging? Is it the feel of it? Is it the idea of it? Is it the emotional associations it has for you? Be clear in your own mind as to what exactly is driving the desire to repeatedly buy something that is directly, or indirectly, derailing your attempts to feel as good as you possibly can. This isn't about labelling foods as good or bad, but rather seeing the movement of the mind.

7. As you wander through the shop, do you find yourself following a particular route, perhaps the same route you've always taken? Use this opportunity to wander down the aisles you would usually ignore. What's there? Are there foods that could potentially be part of your new way of eating? It's worth remembering, if we always do what we've always done, then we'll always get what we've always got.

8. Notice how your route is influenced not only by what you can see, but also by the other senses too. Begin with the physical sensations in the body. For example, do you find yourself hurrying away from the cooler parts of the store, away from the fresh produce, as you try to find somewhere a little warmer? Or do you find yourself feeling agitated and just wanting to get out of the store?

9. Be aware of how your sense of smell influences your route too. For example, do you inexplicably find yourself

in the bread or bakery section of the store? Or perhaps in the fruit area? What is it that's led you there? Is it the smell of the food alone? Or is it the *associations* you have with the smell? So often we make choices based on an idea of what something *might* be like, or *will* be like, rather than what it is *actually* like.

10. Before leaving the shop, remember that (money permitting) you can buy anything you want when you go shopping, you are free to make your own choices. Often the more restrictive our diet becomes, the more conflicting the emotions become. Likewise, the more we suppress feelings of desire, the more they come back again. Only *you* know what foods bring comfort and ease to your body, and calm and clarity to your mind.

HEADSPACE MINDFUL FOOD SHOPPING: EXERCISE 2

This exercise is for when you next go food shopping. Although it is written specifically with the supermarket in mind (simply because that's how most people shop), it can easily be adapted for smaller stores. It's a little more focused and directed than the previous exercise, allowing you to be in and out of the shop without too much dithering, and having made the choices that are right for you. It also assumes that you have completed the Headspace Mindful Food Selection Exercise, and that you have your new shopping list to hand.

1. Begin by choosing a neutral place of focus. This can be the sensation of your feet on the floor, the feeling of the palms resting on the trolley, or the weight of the basket in your hands. This point of focus is going to be your *anchor of awareness* throughout the shopping experience. So this is the place you are going to bring your attention back to when it feels as though the thoughts are running away, or the emotions are spinning off.

2. Remind yourself that this shopping trip is not about trying to control yourself or restrict what you eat. You have the freedom to eat whatever you want. If you can bring this spacious attitude to your food shopping, there'll be a lot less tension in the mind. Also be clear about the foods on the shopping list, and the positive choices you've made beforehand.

3. Move from one item to the next, each time bringing your attention back to your chosen focal point after you've placed the item in your trolley or basket. This is done very gently, almost in a playful way. It's quite normal to feel as though there are too many things vying for your attention (there probably are), which is why it is so important to have one safe place you can come back to each time.

4. Every time you pick something up, remind yourself of the food selection exercise and of the reason you've

chosen to buy that food. If you can, avoid getting caught up in lots of analysis and thinking, instead just make a mental note, an imaginary label if you like, of what the primary reason was for choosing to buy that food. This is really important in terms of reaffirming the positive choices you've made.

5. At times you will find that the mind wanders off. Don't be too concerned about this, but as soon as you realise you've been distracted, just gently bring your attention back to your chosen physical sensation. This applies equally to happy thoughts, sad thoughts, anxious thoughts, thoughts about food, your body, work, home, family, friends – or anything else for that matter. So, each time just readjust your focus in this way.

6. The key to this exercise is to maintain the right amount of effort, naturalness and ease. As a general rule, when we try to do something which we consider to be an important 'task' or 'exercise', we tend to try a bit too hard. This makes the mind very tight, narrow, rigid and inflexible. So remember that this exercise has more to do with *revealing your natural self*, rather than trying to change or reprogramme the mind through force.

7. As you continue to shop, it can be useful to notice how the breath feels in the body. The breath and the mind are intimately connected and it can often be a helpful barometer for how the mind is working. For example,

you may find that as you walk past the chocolate aisle, the breath becomes shorter, or that when you're in the vegetable section it becomes longer. Pause if necessary, taking the time to notice how it feels.

8. As you stand at the till waiting to pay, you will probably be confronted with the usual stack of sweets and chocolate. Now, you can view this as a difficult challenge, your final obstacle, or you can think about it in terms of being a game, of the shop trying to derail your focus from that chosen spot. Remember, each time you realise that the mind has been distracted, just gently bring it back to that spot again.

9. As you focus in that way, remember, there is nobody stopping you from buying these things, no rules that say you are not allowed them. It is simply a case of reflecting 'is this going to help me achieve my ideal size, shape and weight? Is this going to make me feel better about my body? Is this going to improve my relationship with food?' If the answer is no, to even one of these, then it is surely madness to buy them.

10. Before leaving the store, pause briefly on the way out, allowing time for at least one full breath to pass. As you stand there, take a moment to appreciate what you've just done, to feel good about it, and to resolve to do the same each time you go shopping. This is how positive new habits are formed, and the new neural path-

ways that you're creating will benefit greatly from that additional reassurance and affirmation.

MINDFUL FOOD PREPARATION

When I began writing this section, I asked a number of people how long, on average, they spent preparing their food for an evening meal, which for most of us is the main meal of the day. Answers varied from 'How long does it take to unwrap a burger?' to 'About four minutes in the microwave.' Occasionally I'd find someone who still knows how to work an oven, and it seemed that for these people, anything between half an hour and an hour was considered an acceptable amount of time. Now don't panic, I'm not about to ask you to put aside that kind of time each evening, and obviously the preparation, effort, intensity and focus will vary depending on the dish being prepared. But, if we follow the old maxim that it's just as much about the journey as the destination, then clearly the preparation is a very important part of mindful eating.

Where is your mind when you're preparing food usually? I'm not talking about your brain, which I trust is firmly secured in your head. I mean where is your *mind*, your attention? Is the mind busy planning tomorrow's schedule as the knife moves closer and closer towards your fingers along the length of a carrot? Is the mind still wrapped up in some excitement from earlier in the day, replaying a conversation over and over again as you put the rice or pasta on to cook? When we are looking forward to the future or back to the past, then by definition we cannot be in the present.

At first that may not sound so important. But if you think about it, most of the problems we experience as human beings originate in the mind. We tend to get stressed when we think about things, or when we get carried away with emotions. In turn, there is usually then some kind of knock-on effect on our behaviour – whether that's specifically to do with our eating or not. So, the preparation of food actually provides a wonderful opportunity to be present, mindful and aware, as opposed to being distracted, stressed or overwhelmed. It is an opportunity to train the mind, to understand what it means to be in the here and now, with a healthy sense of appreciation, patience, and a nonjudgemental attitude. It's also an opportunity to get back in touch with the food that you eat.

Take a moment to think about the vegetables supplied in your local supermarket. Not so long ago they were just cleaned and put out on the shelf. In fact often they were not even cleaned. But then we became unhappy with the colours and shapes, blemishes and stains. So farmers started to make them brighter, straighter, rounder and altogether easier on the eye. Next came the realisation that if these foods could be washed in advance, then there would be one less thing for us to do at home. And if they were going to wash them for us, then they might as well chop them too, right? Amazingly, for some people that was still not enough, and so came the vegetables that are 'part-cooked', and just need warming up before eating. Now you can walk into a shop and buy sterile plastic bags of washed, peeled, sliced and diced onions, or precooked, ready-to-eat roast potatoes.

In contrast to this, think back to a time when you've handled fresh vegetables, preferably home-grown, or at least local. It might have been when you were a child, or perhaps whilst on holiday in a foreign country. It may have been some fresh tomatoes, an onion, a carrot or some spinach. Whatever it was, there is undeniably something about that kind of produce which looks and feels more natural, which provokes an entirely different response in both body and mind. In an instant we are taken away from the craving for mass-produced, ready-cooked food to a place of innocence, where foods *look* like they should, *feel* like they should, *smell* like they should, *taste* like they should, and yes, even *sound* like they should when we bite into them or cut them with a knife. It's that beautiful moment when you'll hear somebody say, 'Oh yes, *that's* what tomatoes are supposed to taste like.'

Many people I've spoken to say that time is one of the biggest issues when considering the preparation of food. Funnily enough, though, often it has nothing to do with 'not having time', but rather wanting to do something else instead. The preparation is seen as a bit of a chore, as opposed to part of the enjoyment of the meal, so naturally the temptation is to want to do something else instead. It is as if 'prep time' is somehow in competition for 'me time'. But this is an illusion, because any time can be 'me time'. In fact, the only thing that gets in the way of 'me time' is wanting to be somewhere else or to be doing something different. So, if we can be interested, curious and engaged with the preparation of food, then all of a sudden it becomes time well spent, it becomes 'me time'.

For other people it is the sheer monotony, or boredom, of preparing food that is the problem. Compared to our adrena-line-fuelled lives, chopping up a spud or washing salad can feel relatively mundane and a little uneventful. In fact, I'm sure this has driven the demand for ready-prepared meals every bit as much as the time-saving benefits. But it is the simplicity of such an ordinary task that makes it so valuable. It's so delightfully uncomplicated that it requires very little brainpower. Instead it demands just a very gentle awareness, a very balanced effort. And if you can learn to apply this to the preparation of food, then why not to other areas of life too? Mindfulness can be applied anytime, anywhere and to any activity at all. Can you remember a time when you've been so engaged in something that you've forgotten all about the other things you'd rather be doing instead?

Last, but by no means least, if you take the time to mindfully prepare your food, then you can be 100 per cent sure of what's in it. One of the biggest factors in people putting on excess weight is 'hidden calories'. Salads often come drenched in fatty dressings, sandwiches are regularly loaded with so much mayonnaise that they are more calorie-dense than a burger, and so-called 'fat-free' products have a ridiculously high sugar content. Remember, most food manufacturers are not interested in the size of your waistline, they are interested in you eating the foods they want you to eat, and then encouraging you to come back for more. Mindfully preparing your food will ensure that instead you eat only what you want to eat, only what is healthy, and only what is helpful to you in achieving your ideal weight.

HEADSPACE MINDFUL FOOD PREPARATION EXERCISE

For this exercise you can use any food at all, although I'd recommend you use some fresh vegetables or fruit. For the purpose of explaining the exercise I've chosen to use a carrot, some fresh spinach and a fresh tomato, although feel free to exchange these for your own preferred alternatives. As always, you'll get the most from this exercise if you can do it in an environment that is relatively conducive to the task. So, switch your mobile onto silent and ensure there will be as few distractions as possible (at least for the first time you do it, anyway). To begin with it might feel very slow, but that's only because it's the easiest way to learn. Once you've got the hang of the technique, you can simply return to your usual speed of doing things, only this time with a lot more awareness. You can do this sitting down or standing up, however you prefer.

1. Before you wash, cut or peel anything, take a good look at what it is you are about to prepare, cook and eat. As strange as it may sound, we often don't really see things for what they are. Instead we look at them with a projection of what we think we *should* see. By reconnecting with the foods in this way you are actually reconnecting your mind (your neural pathways) with more positive patterns of behaviour and perception.

2. Moving towards the sink, run the different vegetables under the tap, gently removing any dirt or dust. Notice the temperature of the water, the different textures of the vegetables and even any smells. Let go of any thoughts for just a minute or two, as you focus your attention wholeheartedly on the temperature, textures and smells.

3. As you're washing the vegetables, you may well find that thoughts just keep coming back. You might find yourself planning the next day, or running through a conversation in your mind, perhaps one that hasn't even happened yet. Or maybe you're thinking about what you'd rather be doing instead. Whatever it is, as soon as you realise the mind has wandered off, gently bring your attention back to the sense of touch.

4. Next place the vegetables on a chopping board in front of you. Begin by picking up the carrot. Even if you don't usually peel carrots, on this occasion take a knife or a peeler and slowly begin to peel. As you do so, take the time to be present with the physical sensations. Notice how the carrot looks, how it smells, how it feels and even how it sounds as the knife cuts through the skin. Try to resist tasting it just yet, though.

5. As you're doing this, try to be aware of those subtle feelings of satisfaction, pleasure, boredom or restlessness, or whatever feeling is most apparent. Only when you can see your thoughts and feelings clearly will you feel fully in control of your diet. When you've finished peeling the carrot, chop it the way you'd like to, being aware of both the sounds and also the physical sensation of the arm and hand as it moves the knife.

6. Something you might find really useful is to monitor your levels of effort as you chop, and indeed

throughout the entire process. For example, do you find yourself struggling to chop the vegetables, or are you pushing so hard that you threaten to go through the chopping board as well? This will usually give you a good indication of your state of mind. You can then put the carrots in a bowl, keeping one piece aside to taste later on.

7. Next up is the spinach. Take hold of a bunch and cut it in half with the knife, smelling it afterwards. Does it smell sweet, bitter, fresh, stale? The more interested and genuinely curious you are about this process, the more you'll see, the more you'll discover, and the more you'll understand about the dynamics of your mind. It's not about thinking, it's about being aware. Place one piece aside to eat later, and put the rest in a bowl.

8. Finally, take hold of the tomato and bring it to your nose. If the tomato is fresh and naturally produced it should have a wonderful smell. Take the time to feel the texture of the tomato as well, before cutting it in half, and then into quarters. Apply as little effort as possible to this process. And then, once again, pick it up, smell it, touch it, look at it, be interested. As before, then place one piece aside and the rest in a bowl.

9. Sitting down at the table, place the three pieces you put aside in front of you. There should just be a small

amount of each, no more than a mouthful. As you look at them together, notice how radically different they are from each other, how the colours contrast, how the textures differ, how they smell so differently from one another.

10. Finally, taste each one, taking the time to notice the flavours. This is an important element of preparing food, ensuring you know what you are about to cook and how it will be best prepared. Does it need additional flavouring; does it need frying, grilling, baking and so on? Really pay attention to each flavour. Take the time to really appreciate each and every food you're preparing to cook.

MINDFUL COOKING

Many of the aspects mentioned in the mindful preparation of food apply equally to the mindful cooking of food. However, there are a few additional factors. For example, what does it usually look like in the kitchen when you've finished the cooking? Does it look as though a bomb has gone off, with ingredients halfway up the wall, pots stacked precariously on top of each other, and a smoke alarm detector hanging from the ceiling having been beaten into submission by the heel of your shoe? Or are you the kind of person who likes to tidy as they go, possibly a Calorie Counter, methodically working from one thing to the next? It's quite possible to remain aware throughout either scenario, but there is no question that it is easier and more pleasant to be mindful and calm in the latter environment.

Have you ever noticed what it's like to cook something you've never tried before? Usually there is an element of excitement, of interest, or curiosity. If we are cooking for others as well, we might even throw a bit of anxiety into the mix. But mostly there is the anticipation of what it's going to taste like. In fact, some people get so carried away with this anticipation that they've mentally eaten the dish before it has even come out of the oven. But what about during the cooking process itself? Where is your mind? Where is your attention? Do you tend to feel relaxed and at ease, or stressed-out and impatient?

I remember when I was learning the fundamentals of mindful eating in the first monastery I trained at in the Himalayas. We were encouraged to be present in the kitchen throughout the entire cooking process (and not just physically), even if there was nothing to do and the dish required several hours in the oven. The idea was to be interested and at ease with whatever was going on at the time. During the cooking process, this meant engaging the senses of sound and smell primarily, effectively using them as a point of focus. Whilst I'm not suggesting you spend hours in your kitchen at home in quite the same way, it can be a really revealing exercise (so much so that I've included a shorter version at the end of this section).

For example, lasagne cooking in the oven smells like . . . lasagne, right? Well, yes and no. If you are really alert to the senses then you can actually smell each of the ingredients as they begin to cook, rather than the lasagne as a whole. You can also smell the flavours developing and deepening as they begin to mix and complement each other. It is an incredible thing to discover, free from any distraction, being present with each and every part of the process. The same can be said of any food, even cold foods. It is no different to tasting wine, chocolate or cheese, where even the most subtle flavours, scents and textures can be identified if the attention is placed squarely on the senses. You might also become increasingly aware of your appetite starting to build as the smells of the food begin to activate all the relevant systems in the body. This will usually happen regardless of whether we actually need the food or not.

Of course, most family kitchens are quite busy places. We often have other people around, children playing, babies screaming, partners talking. Many kitchens now even have TVs on the wall, digital radios built into the appliances, and 'cooking time' is increasingly seen as an opportunity to catch up with a few phone calls. In fact, it's this section of the population that keeps chiropractors in business; cradling the phone between their ear and shoulder as they pace around in the kitchen, their head becomes permanently stuck at a 45-degree angle. Obviously there are limits as to how much we can prevent potential distractions, but one thing we can be sure about: the more chaotic it is on the outside, the more chaotic it is likely to be on the inside. So, taking practical steps to reduce the amount of noise and confusion whilst cooking can only be a good thing.

HEADSPACE MINDFUL COOKING EXERCISE

There are many different ways of doing this exercise, depending on the type of food being cooked and the method being employed to cook it. For example, if it is an oven baked dish, then you have nothing to do but sit back and remain alert to your senses as you gently focus on the breath. But if you are boiling, grilling or frying then you're going to need to remain somewhat active and involved, as you stir, shake, flip or fry. So I've included two short exercises here – choose the one that seems to fit best.

Remember, to get the most from these exercises it is a good idea to switch off your phone and remove any other potential distraction from the kitchen (where possible and appropriate). Once you've got the hang of how to do it, you'll soon be able to apply the technique just as well with other people around and with noise in the background.

Slow Cooking (Little to Do)

1. Placing the food in the oven, grill or casserole, set the heat, the timer, and make sure there is nothing else you need to think about.

2. Sit in a chair not too far from the oven or hob and relax into it. You have nothing to do but to stay alert to the changing sounds, smells, sensations and thoughts as you gently focus your attention on the breath. Try it just for a few minutes at a time to begin with, perhaps returning to the kitchen every 10–15 minutes or so to repeat the exercise and notice the changes.

3. There's no need to worry if your mind wanders off whilst you're doing this, but as soon as you realise it's wandered, just bring your attention back to the breath. Having done so, then shift your attention to the other

senses, such as the smell, the increasingly warm temperature in the room, or the rumbling in your stomach as the digestive juices begin to flow in preparation for the meal.

4. Be as accurate as you can in recognising the different smells, fragrances, flavours and foods as they cook. It is as if you are trying to pick up every last scent, every last nuance. It is surprising just how much you can recognise when you really put your mind to it.

5. As you become aware of these things, notice where your mind wants to travel. Does it drift off to memories past, perhaps associating the smells with previous meals? Or does it race ahead to the future, perhaps imagining what the food is going to taste like? This doesn't require any analysis or thinking, it is simply a matter of being aware.

Fast Cooking (Lots to Do)

1. Begin from the very first moment you place the water on the heat, or pour the oil in the pan. Listen to the sounds, the smells, and the sensations that the heat immediately gives rise to.

2. As you begin to cook the various foods, notice how the addition of each new ingredient affects the overall fragrance of the dish. Allow yourself to be 100 per cent present with the different physical senses, rather than

being lost in thought. Each time the mind wanders, just gently bring the attention back to these sounds and smells.

3. Try to be aware of how your mood and your thinking changes throughout the cooking process. Do you find the heat oppressive? Do you find yourself getting anxious trying to keep all the different things going at once, or confident and in control? Don't try and change any of these things for now – simply building up a picture is enough.

4. As you observe the mind, use the physical senses as a safe place to come back to when you feel the emotions running off. For example, rather than feeling anxious about feeling anxious, come back to the smell of the food, and instead of getting increasingly frustrated at feeling frustrated, bring your attention back to the sounds of the food cooking.

5. Throughout this exercise, notice how your mind behaves. Is it a mind that's comfortable being in the moment? Or does it tend to constantly race off to plan things for the future, or drift off to memories of the past? Being aware of the thoughts in this way will help you to get much better at the exercise, which for most people means enjoying an altogether more serene experience in the kitchen.

MINDFUL EATING

And so to the heart of this entire exercise – the main course, if you will. Whilst all of the other aspects of mindful eating will undoubtedly enhance your experience of eating, help to improve your relationship with food, whilst significantly increasing the potential for reaching your ideal weight, it is with the process of eating itself that things really begin to change. This is where you are likely to see the biggest shift and the most obvious link between a calm and steady mind and a manageable and healthy diet.

There is a famous old Zen proverb that says, 'When you sit, just sit, when you walk, just walk, and when you eat, just eat.' I think it would be fair to say that very few people live this way. When we sit we tend to find ways to occupy ourselves, to keep the mind busy. It can feel so alien to just stop and do nothing. This is why an exercise like Take10 is so important. It helps you to become more familiar with that feeling of 'just sitting', to be at ease with it. The same is true of eating: very few people 'just eat'. Most people like to talk, listen to music, watch TV, use the computer, or read a book or a magazine. When was the last time you sat down at a table and 'just ate'? As I say, at first it can be unnerving to 'just sit' or 'just eat', but with a little practice it will become a genuinely pleasant experience and, just as importantly, an excellent way of managing your eating.

People often assume that eating mindfully simply means to slow down and do it very carefully, but this isn't the case. Doing something carefully and being mindful are two different things. In the same way that you can apply awareness equally to walking slowly along a garden path, or sprinting flat out around an athletics track, you can be mindful whilst enjoying a leisurely meal at home, or grabbing a sandwich on the fly whilst out and about. It's just that in becoming more aware, you will soon discover that wolfing down a snack in between emails or, worse, whilst racing down the street, doesn't really feel so good. The body is so much better at digesting foods when it is in one place, when the mind is calm and the emotions are stable. In fact, there is a good amount of research to show that these factors even influence the amount of nutrients absorbed by the body.

Of course, chewing every mouthful of food thoroughly is not a new idea, and if you're anything like most people, you will have been encouraged to do this from a young age. In the past there were diets – and even entire movements – created around the go-slow approach to chewing food. But right now it's the scientific community who are interested in the speed at which we eat our food. That's because research is starting to show that when we slow down our eating, and take the time to chew each mouthful thoroughly, we eat less food. It sounds so obvious, and yet few of us actually remember to do it. One company in Scandinavia think they've got the answer to this problem and have recently started selling plates that recognise the speed you're eating at and tell you to slow down if you're going too fast! Whether you choose to eat this way is of course entirely up to you, but if it helps you to appreciate the food more, whilst eating less, then it would seem to make a great deal of sense.

Another common assumption is that mindful eating has to be done alone, with nobody else around, in complete silence and retreat-like conditions. Whilst there's no doubt it's easier to learn with fewer distractions, mindful eating can be done anywhere. No matter whether you are eating at home with the children, snacking with colleagues at work, having lunch alone in a busy café, or dinner out with friends, mindful eating can be applied to each and every one of these environments. But when you are learning the traditional technique, I would suggest you do it alone, at least for the first few times. It's for this reason I've included a second exercise below, for when you are eating with others. It has a slightly different emphasis and encourages you to engage the mind in a different way. This means you can start your mindful eating straight away, no matter what your circumstances.

HEADSPACE MINDFUL EATING EXERCISE

As important as all the other exercises are in this book, the technique of mindful eating outlined below is arguably one of the most important. This is the moment when you are likely to feel most physically and mentally engaged with the food. Although I've explained it in a traditional way here, and have encouraged you to try it alone and sitting at a table, that's only to make it easier to learn. Once you feel confident in applying the principles in this context, then you'll be able to do it anywhere, regardless of whether you're on your own or with others.

1. Sit down at a table, preferably alone, and free from any external distractions. Don't worry too much if there are sounds that are out of your control; you can build these into the exercise in the same way as you did with

Take10. Before you even pick up the food to eat, take a couple of deep breaths – in through the nose and out through the mouth – just to allow the body and mind to settle.

2. Next, take a moment to appreciate the food. Where has it come from? What country? Was it grown or was it manufactured? Try and imagine the different ingredients in their natural growing environment and even the types of people who would have been looking after the crops or animals. By reconnecting with these simple facts you will begin to make better choices and move closer to your desired goals.

3. As you're doing this, notice if there is any sense of impatience in the mind, of wanting to get on and eat the food. Perhaps you're thinking of all the things you need to do. Whatever the reaction, it's most likely just conditioned behaviour, a habit, but one which you may well find surprisingly strong. Regardless of the feeling, take at least a minute to reflect in this way.

4. Next, without going on some kind of guilt trip, take a moment to appreciate the fact that you actually have food on your plate. We're so familiar with this situation that we forget that for many people in the world, this just isn't the case. A deep sense of appreciation and gratitude is at the heart of any stable mindfulness practice.

5. If it's a food you're going to eat with the hands, then notice the texture as you pick it up, the temperature, and perhaps the colour(s). If it's from a plate with a knife and fork, notice instead the texture and temperature of the cutlery as you move it towards the food, but still take the time to notice the colours on the plate. You might find it more effective to hold your fork or spoon in your less dominant hand, as this will prevent you from going too quickly.

6. As you move the food towards your mouth, shift the focus away from the hands and more towards the eyes, nose and mouth. How does the food smell? What does it look like up close? And, as you put it in your mouth, what is the taste, the texture, the temperature? You don't need to 'do' anything. You're simply observing the different bodily senses at work.

7. In addition to the physical senses, notice how the mind responds to the food. For example, is the food met with pleasure or displeasure in your mind? Is there acceptance of the food as it is, or maybe some resistance to certain aspects of it? Perhaps it's too hot, too cold, too sweet, or too sour. Notice how the mind rushes to judge the food and to make comparisons with previous meals or other possibilities. Whatever you do, take the time to chew the food fully. Not only is this a healthier way of eating, but it will allow you the time to taste and appreciate all the different flavours.

8. Once you've taken a few mouthfuls, you may well find that the mind starts to get bored of the exercise and will wander off into thinking about something else. As with Take10, this is quite normal and nothing to worry about. So, in just the same way as before, as soon as you realise it's wandered off, gently bring your attention back to the process of eating, and the different tastes, smells, textures, sights and sounds.

9. As you continue to eat your meal in this way, you can start to notice whether there's a strong habitual urge to eat more quickly (perhaps to move closer to dessert!). Or maybe there are feelings of unease about what you're eating. If it's an especially big meal, you may even notice the desire to consume gradually decreasing as the stomach becomes full and you become more aware of these sensations. As much as possible, simply observe these different thoughts and feelings (obviously acting on them where appropriate) and, if you can, notice how the breath appears as well. The breath may well give you some indication of how comfortable or uncomfortable the process of eating is for you.

10. Before jumping up to get on with the next thing you have planned, try just staying seated for a moment or two. This is an opportunity for you to take that sense of being present to the next part of your day. It's an opportunity to realise that the thoughts, feelings and physical sensations that were present before eating

have now moved on. In time, this awareness of change can help the mind to feel more spacious and at ease.

HEADSPACE MINDFUL EATING EXERCISE (WITH OTHERS)

1. Remember, there are no rules as to what you can or can't eat, so you have no need to feel anxious or worried in advance about what you can have. It is not about having an iron will that can resist anything, but rather a soft and flexible approach that is skilful.

2. If you are ordering food from a menu, clearly picture the food in your mind before ordering it. Remember where it comes from, how it tastes and, most importantly, how it's made you feel afterwards when you've eaten it before.

3. If you are eating at a friend's house or with your family, then you may well find that you have no choice as to what you are going to eat. In these situations your focus might be more to do with portion sizes and number of helpings rather than the food itself. Remind yourself that you are there primarily to enjoy and share in the company of others. This will often soften the mind and help put things into perspective.

4. If you can, begin to notice quite early on how the mind is behaving. Remember, there is no 'should' or 'shouldn't', so allow all the thoughts of desire (and possibly of resistance) to just come and go. These are perfectly normal, and just because a thought appears in the mind, it doesn't mean you have to follow through with it.

5. You might find this easier if you have a physical sensation to focus on in your body. You don't have to keep your attention there the whole time, but it is a place to come back to, to focus on, when you feel as though the mind is spinning off. The sensation of the feet on the floor or the body against the chair seems to work well for most people. This is done very gently, alongside conversation and eating.

6. Check in with your breath every now and then if you can. The breath will often reflect the mind, and so when the thoughts and emotions become very excited, the breath will often become quite shallow and faint. There's no need to alter your breathing in any way: simply becoming more aware of it will help. Subtly placing your hand on your stomach can often help you to get more in touch with this feeling.

7. Without it being forced, try to remain engaged with whatever is being said. Essentially this means listening and being interested in what others have to say. This is

in contrast to your mind wandering off to what emails you need to send or to the cheesecake you caught a glimpse of earlier. If your attention is truly with the other person, then it can't be somewhere else with feelings of anxiety or thoughts of weight loss.

8. Notice how the choices of others influence both how you think and how you feel. Rather than getting swept up and being affected by these choices, simply acknowledge them for what they are and remain present with your own desired choices. Any short-term feelings of missing out will be more than compensated for by the positive feelings of wellbeing and confidence you'll experience afterwards.

9. Be aware of how alcohol influences and affects your decisions as well. There is nothing wrong with enjoying a few drinks amongst friends, but if it consistently undermines and derails your attempts to live and eat as you'd like to, then you have to question the wisdom of such an approach. Perhaps try to discover at what point you usually lose your way and then, next time, stop one drink short of that.

10. Last, but by no means least, don't take yourself too seriously. There is something a little uncomfortable for all concerned when a member of the group puts their foot down. If friends try to persuade you to eat something you'd rather not, have a laugh about it, joke

about it, and yet gently maintain your position. Mindful eating is about having a relaxed sense of focus, rather than developing the usual militant approach to eating and dieting.

CHAPTER NINE

THE HEADSPACE 10-DAY PLAN

INTRODUCTION

As I said at the beginning of this book, it is only when you *apply* mindfulness to life that it becomes useful; it is only when you *eat* mindfully that you can start to make genuine changes to your eating habits, the relationship you have with your body, and to the outer appearance of that body. The next 10 days is the beginning of something that has the potential to change your life. With that in mind, this chapter is incredibly important. It is the meat in your mindfulness sandwich (or the textured-vegetable-protein-meat-substitute, if you're that way inclined).

It's likely to be very different to what you're used to, because this is not a diet as such. I won't be telling you what foods you can and can't eat. Most of you will be only too well aware of which foods promote health, esteem and feelings of wellbeing, and which foods (when abused) lead towards weight gain, conflicting emotions and heart disease. Besides, mindful eating is about encouraging a greater sense of confidence and trust in your own decision-making abilities. It's about giving up the crutch of dependency and feeling in control of the choices you make. It is about putting the responsibility for what you eat back into your hands. But if you would still like some general guidance on what foods to include in your 10-Day Plan, then you can find some nutritional recommendations in the next chapter.

Needless to say, a balanced diet including all the major food groups is key to the success of this programme. Carbohydrates are not the enemy, there's no need to cut out fat altogether. Neither is it a diet of calorie counting, ready-prepared weight-loss meals, or special powdered formulas. These types of diets are simply unsustainable. And even if they weren't, is that really the way you want to live the rest of your life – eating foods designed for astronauts? Is that approach really going to give you peace of mind? Wouldn't it be nice to be able to relax with food, to enjoy it, to appreciate it, and yet still reach or maintain your ideal weight, shape and size? Wouldn't it be nice to understand the different processes at play for yourself, to understand why you eat, what you eat, and when you eat? Wouldn't it be good to be fully in control of your eating habits and at ease with the size and shape of your body?

In many ways, mindful eating is deceptive in its simplicity. At first glance this eating plan may appear surprisingly straightforward, nothing but good old fashioned common sense, perhaps lacking the exoticism of some faddish diets. But there is nothing remotely 'common' about any of the information in this book, because if the techniques were 'common' then we'd all be living this way – which is clearly not the case. However, the fact remains that, just like so many other things in life, it is often the most simple and straightforward approaches that bring about the best results, and mindful eating is no exception. In fact it remains as one of the most authentic, effective and transformative behavioural change techniques ever discovered.

But this 1o-Day Plan will require your attention, it will *demand* your attention, as you become more and more familiar with shifting your focus back to the here and now. Remember, mindfulness is a skill just like any other and it requires practice. You shouldn't expect to get it right every time to begin with. When you are learning, it takes a little more effort to remember everything, but before long it will become second nature. In a world where so many things are vying for our attention, it can be difficult to focus on just one. But this really does come back to your priorities and your motivation. If you want to see a significant difference and experience a sustainable shift, then that means sticking with the plan each and every day. It means being *interested* in your eating habits, *curious* about your thought patterns, and *inspired* about the potential of lasting change.

With this in mind, there are a few simple guidelines that will help you to get the very best from the next 10 days. It doesn't matter whether you're sitting down for dinner or grabbing a snack on the go, these guidelines apply equally.

MINDFUL EATING: RULES OF ENGAGEMENT

1. Remember the approach

As long as you follow the guidance of the plan, you can eat anything you want over the next 10 days. Whilst it's a good idea to follow the general recommended guidelines in the next chapter to get the best results, it's not helpful to bring a narrow way of thinking and inflexible approach to the plan. Mindful eating is about *understanding* the mind, rather than trying to control it, or overcome it in some way.

2. Clear out the cupboards

Changing lifelong eating habits is hard enough as it is, so make things as easy as you can to begin with. Give away any foods that you feel are in conflict with your new way of eating or desired weight-loss goals. Peace of mind and acceptance can sometimes be as simple as knowing there isn't any more chocolate left in the cupboard.

3. Reflect before you shop

Before walking into a shop, be clear about what you're going in there to buy. You can still appreciate all the other things in the shop, but this way you'll only be shopping for the things that you actually *need* and intended to buy, rather than the things you just happen to come across whilst shopping. Oh, and remember not to do your food shopping when you're hungry.

4. Breathe before you buy

Impulse purchases are where most people go wrong. So, if it feels as though you're about to buy something you'll later regret, rather than try and talk your way out of it (or into it), try the following. Wait for your body to exhale. Don't force it, just wait for it to exhale, all the way, to the very end of the breath. If you have time, wait for another breath to follow. See if you still feel the same about buying the food now.

5. Pause before you eat

It doesn't matter why, the important thing is that you pause long enough for the mind to settle and for the emotions to become clear. It might be a pause to reflect on where the food has come from, to see whether you are actually hungry, or to simply appreciate and be thankful that there's food on the plate. A very minimum of 10 seconds is a must every time for this one.

6. Sit to eat your food

Whenever possible, sit down at a table to eat your food, even if it is only a snack. At the very least, sit down *somewhere* to eat your food. It is simply unrealistic to expect a mindful eating plan to work effectively if you are shovelling a sandwich down your throat as you run along the street chasing after a friend.

7. Limit distractions

There is a good reason why cinemas are generally quiet places and free from distraction. The quiet enables you to focus on the film, to enjoy it, to appreciate it, to understand what's going on. The same is true of food and the mind. When you're learning to eat mindfully, it is far more challenging if you're trying to do 10 things at once. So, keep things to a minimum when you are doing any of the exercises included in the plan.

8. Remain curious

No matter how many times you've eaten this *type* of food, it is not the *same* food. So leave behind any memories of previous meals and avoid projecting old ideas on to new experiences. As much as possible, approach every eating experience over the next 10 days with the same curiosity that you would bring to trying something completely new.

9. Engage the senses

Although the plan encourages you to focus on specific physical senses at certain times, make it your goal to acknowledge all five senses at every meal. For example, there are some foods (processed in particular) that on closer examination you probably wouldn't eat at all. So, make a mental checklist and acknowledge all five senses every time you eat.

10. Walk away

Sometimes thoughts and emotions around food can arise so quickly, and feel so overwhelming, that's it's almost impossible to have any calm or clarity. The body doesn't digest things well when the mind is stirred up, and it's much more difficult to be mindful, so take a step back from it all, walk away if necessary, and return once the mind has settled.

HOW TO USE THE MINDFUL EATING DIET 10-DAY PLAN

Over the next 10 days you will begin to see the true benefits of being more mindful. For example, you will learn how to engage the senses before, during and after eating; you will learn how to see thoughts about food and your body with clarity, and without getting swept away by them; you will learn about your emotions and their importance in following a healthy diet; you will learn how to listen to the body, what it likes, what it doesn't like, what it needs, and what it doesn't need; and you will begin to see, perhaps for the very first time, why you follow the patterns of behaviour that you do. This is what it means to listen to your natural intelligence, to be mindful and aware. It doesn't happen overnight, but evolves and develops over time. So, remember that mindful eating is not meant to be something temporary, but is designed to be a new way of eating for life!

As you can see from the plan, each day consists of five distinct eating times, to be incorporated into your own daily routine at times that best suit you. The plan will undoubtedly provide the best results if you don't eat outside of those times. I appreciate that five times a day might sound like a lot to many people (and possibly not much at all to others), but remember we are still talking about just three *meals* a day (with healthy sized portions), but with an additional two small, healthy snacks. This is really important for maintaining a steady blood-sugar level and will help to control feelings of hunger, stabilise emotions, and actually reduce the risk of snacking or bingeing on unhealthy foods between meal times (or even *at* meal times).

Once again, please remember, this is not a diet, and if you are not sure what foods promote health and wellbeing, or the portion sizes you should be using for each meal or snack, take a look at the Headspace Handy Guide to Nutrition in the next chapter.

Now, whilst it may sound a little old-fashioned, I'm also going to ask you to keep a track of what you eat in a food journal that is incorporated into the plan. This can be really useful in looking back and assessing your physical, emotional and mental state in relation to specific foods. In fact, for each meal and snack you will be encouraged to investigate your physical, emotional and mental state – before, during and after the food. You will also be asked to engage the senses, to become aware of your level of hunger, to assess how you feel, and to notice whether your mind is in a state of clarity or confusion, calm or unrest. Being open and aware of these things is essential. It is this curious, interested and objective approach that will enable you to see your relationships with food and the body in a whole new way. And it is this new perspective that will allow genuine, sustainable change to take place.

THE BODY

The Senses

At each meal you will be asked to focus on one specific sense. This is not meant to be at the exclusion of all other senses, or indeed any thoughts and feelings, but what it does mean is that this one sense will be your primary focal point. If you find your mind wandering off elsewhere, remember to gently bring your attention back to whichever one of the five physical senses you are being encouraged to use at that time.

The Five Physical Senses

1. Taste
2. Touch
3. Sight
4. Smell
5. Hearing

Hunger

In an extension to engaging the senses, and to help you become more aware and in tune with feelings of hunger, you will also be asked to rate your level of hunger before and after each meal. It might also be helpful to rate it midway through your meal too, just for your own interest, but no need to write that one down.

Take a look to see how you feel and write the corresponding number in the box provided at each meal.

The Headspace Hunger Rating

1. Starving

(weak, dizzy, and quite possibly beyond the point of feeling hungry)

2. Ravenous

(very uncomfortable, irritable, low energy, possible headache)

3. Very hungry

(stomach rumbling, feelings of desire, totally preoccupied with food)

4. Slightly hungry

(thoughts drifting towards food, subtle sensations of hunger)

5. Neutral

(neither a feeling of hunger or fullness)

6. Slightly full

(pleasantly satisfied, awareness of having eaten, comfortable sensation)

7. Very full

(bordering on over-full, loss of appetite, uncomfortable sensation)

8. Stuffed

(belt-loosening territory, tired, lethargic and stomach painfully stretched)

9. Nauseous

(strong aversion to food, feelings of sickness, painful sensations of bloating)

10. Medical attention

(time to call a doctor!)

THE THINKING MIND

Whilst the mind incorporates both thought and feeling in equal measure, for the purposes of this book (and you getting the maximum benefit from it), I have separated the mind into two categories: The Thinking Mind and The Emotional Mind. This is a distinction commonly made in scientific trials, with the former relating specifically to rumination, or thinking, and the latter applying to feelings, or emotions.

Before and after each meal you will be asked to provide a rating for how you experience your thinking mind, both in terms of mind chatter and clarity. Mind chatter relates to the relative feeling of calm or restlessness in the mind – whether there are lots of thoughts, or none at all. The Clarity Rating, on the other hand, has more to do with how clear you are about your goals and intentions, your decision-making ability, and noticing how certain foods can leave you feeling a particular way.

Take a look at the following scales to assess your experience and then write the corresponding number in the box provided at each meal.

The Headspace Mind Chatter Rating

1. Silence
(nothing, not a thing, *nada*, like nothing you have ever known)

2. Extremely calm
(blissfully quiet, you could hear a pin drop, very few thoughts)

3. Very calm
(unusually quiet, infrequent thoughts, a feeling of stillness)

4. Fairly calm
(pleasantly quiet, very little mind wandering, few thoughts)

5. Neutral
(neither a strong feeling of calm or of restlessness)

6. Slightly restless
(occasional mind wandering, difficulty in getting comfortable)

7. Very restless
(frequent thoughts, tendency to look for distraction, physically agitated)

8. Extremely restless
(constant mind chatter, severe agitation, craving distraction)

9. Incapacitated
(relentless thinking, physically exhausted, unable to engage in activity)

10. Aaaaargh!
(irresistible urge to bang head against wall – please don't!)

The Headspace Clarity Rating

1. Crystal clear
(laser-like focus, like watching the mind in slow motion – in HD!)

2. Extremely clear
(very focused, conscious of intention, effortless decision-making)

3. Very clear
(emotions easily identifiable, decisions easy to make, sense of perspective)

4. Quite clear
(awareness of habitual patterns, potential to respond skilfully)

5. Neutral
(neither a strong feeling of clarity or confusion)

6. Slightly confused
(trace of uncertainty, emotions hazy, intentions unstable)

7. Very confused
(emotions unidentifiable, decision-making difficult, feeling of conflict)

8. Extremely confused
(overwhelmed by emotion, loss of perspective, unskilful actions)

9. Blissfully unaware
(not even aware of being unaware, total and utter confusion reigns)

10. What's my name?
(time to Take1o!)

THE EMOTIONAL MIND

Before and after each meal or snack you will be asked to write down how you are feeling, by selecting an emotion from the Headspace Tracker you can see on page 202. Many people find this difficult at first, mostly because they are usually too caught up in the emotion itself to see it for what it is. However, with just a little practice it will become second nature.

Sometimes you might be aware of more than one emotion. If this is the case, simply write down the emotion which feels strongest. And don't worry if the exact emotion that you're feeling is not listed on the wheel. In the context of this exercise it is quite OK to write down the emotion that is *closest* to the way that you're feeling.

Looking at the Headspace Tracker, you'll see that the groupings are split into four distinct areas, each with four examples of emotions that fall in that particular category. This is based on an emotional scale and language that is commonly used in mindfulness-based psychological studies.

I don't think it's helpful (or accurate) to see emotions as positive or negative, as that requires a subjectivity that in many ways is in contrast to the objectivity promoted by mindfulness.

However, in the interests of explaining this in an easy and accessible way, I will refer to relatively 'positive' and 'negative' emotional states as they are perceived and experienced by most people.

Here's how it all breaks down, moving around the wheel in a clockwise direction:

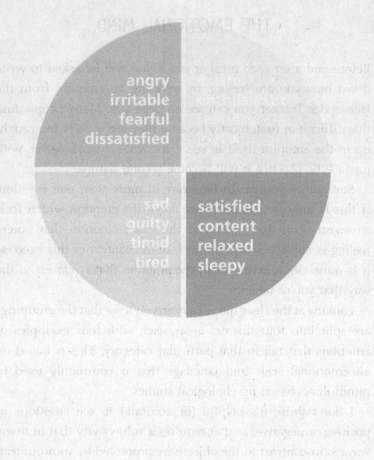

Top Right Quadrant

This section of the wheel suggests a relatively positive state of mind, which is lively, energetic and dynamic in nature. In short, the emotions here reflect a wide range of dynamic positivity.

The four emotions in this quadrant are excited, enthusiastic, fearless and joyful.

Bottom Right Quadrant

This section of the wheel suggests a relatively positive state of mind, which is less active, less energetic, and calmer in nature. In short, the emotions here reflect a wide range of calm positivity.

The four emotions in this quadrant are satisfied, content, relaxed and sleepy.

Bottom Left Quadrant

This section of the wheel suggests a relatively negative state of mind, which is less active, less energetic, and subdued in nature. In short, the emotions here reflect a wide range of subdued negativity.

The four emotions in this quadrant are sad, guilty, timid and tired.

Top Left Quadrant

This section of the wheel suggests a relatively negative state of mind, which is lively, energetic and dynamic in nature. In short, the emotions here reflect a wide range of dynamic negativity.

The four emotions in this quadrant are angry, irritable, fearful and dissatisfied.

DAY 1

. . . .

Breakfast: _____

Before Eating   emotion: _____
Hunger rating .... [   ]   _____
Mind chatter rating..... [   ]   _____
Clarity rating.......... [   ]   _____

After Eating   emotion: _____
Hunger rating.......... [   ]   _____
Mind chatter rating..... [   ]   _____
Clarity rating.......... [   ]   _____

. . . .

Snack: _____

Before Eating   emotion: _____
Hunger rating.......... [   ]   _____
Mind chatter rating..... [   ]   _____
Clarity rating.......... [   ]   _____

After Eating   emotion: _____
Hunger rating.......... [   ]   _____
Mind chatter rating..... [   ]   _____
Clarity rating.......... [   ]   _____

. . . .

Lunch: _____

Before Eating   emotion: _____
Hunger rating.......... [   ]   _____
Mind chatter rating..... [   ]   _____
Clarity rating.......... [   ]   _____

After Eating   emotion: _____
Hunger rating.......... [   ]   _____
Mind chatter rating..... [   ]   _____
Clarity rating.......... [   ]   _____

Snack: _____

Before Eating   emotion: _____

Hunger rating.......... [   ]

Mind chatter rating..... [   ]

Clarity rating.......... [   ]

After Eating   emotion: _____

Hunger rating.......... [   ]

Mind chatter rating..... [   ]

Clarity rating.......... [   ]

Dinner: _____

Before Eating   emotion: _____

Hunger rating.......... [   ]

Mind chatter rating..... [   ]

Clarity rating.......... [   ]

After Eating   emotion: _____

Hunger rating.......... [   ]

Mind chatter rating..... [   ]

Clarity rating.......... [   ]

Reflection:

_____

_____

_____

_____

_____

_____

_____

DAY 2

....

Breakfast: _____

Before Eating   emotion: _____

Hunger rating.......... [   ] _____
Mind chatter rating..... [   ] _____
Clarity rating.......... [   ] _____

After Eating   emotion: _____

Hunger rating.......... [   ] _____
Mind chatter rating..... [   ] _____
Clarity rating.......... [   ] _____

....

Snack: _____

Before Eating   emotion: _____

Hunger rating.......... [   ] _____
Mind chatter rating..... [   ] _____
Clarity rating.......... [   ] _____

After Eating   emotion: _____

Hunger rating.......... [   ] _____
Mind chatter rating..... [   ] _____
Clarity rating.......... [   ] _____

....

Lunch: _____

Before Eating   emotion: _____

Hunger rating.......... [   ] _____
Mind chatter rating..... [   ] _____
Clarity rating.......... [   ] _____

After Eating   emotion: _____

Hunger rating.......... [   ] _____
Mind chatter rating..... [   ] _____
Clarity rating.......... [   ] _____

Snack: _____

_____

Before Eating   emotion: _____
Hunger rating.......... [   ]
Mind chatter rating..... [   ]
Clarity rating.......... [   ]

After Eating   emotion: _____
Hunger rating.......... [   ]
Mind chatter rating..... [   ]
Clarity rating.......... [   ]

Dinner: _____

_____

Before Eating   emotion: _____
Hunger rating.......... [   ]
Mind chatter rating..... [   ]
Clarity rating.......... [   ]

After Eating   emotion: _____
Hunger rating.......... [   ]
Mind chatter rating..... [   ]
Clarity rating.......... [   ]

Reflection:

_____

_____

_____

_____

_____

_____

_____

DAY 3

. . . .

Breakfast: _____

Before Eating   emotion: _____
Hunger rating.......... [   ]   _____
Mind chatter rating..... [   ]   _____
Clarity rating.......... [   ]   _____

After Eating   emotion: _____
Hunger rating.......... [   ]   _____
Mind chatter rating..... [   ]   _____
Clarity rating.......... [   ]   _____

. . . .

Snack: _____

Before Eating   emotion: _____
Hunger rating.......... [   ]   _____
Mind chatter rating..... [   ]   _____
Clarity rating.......... [   ]   _____

After Eating   emotion: _____
Hunger rating.......... [   ]   _____
Mind chatter rating..... [   ]   _____
Clarity rating.......... [   ]   _____

. . . .

Lunch: _____

Before Eating   emotion: _____
Hunger rating.......... [   ]   _____
Mind chatter rating..... [   ]   _____
Clarity rating.......... [   ]   _____

After Eating   emotion: _____
Hunger rating.......... [   ]   _____
Mind chatter rating..... [   ]   _____
Clarity rating.......... [   ]   _____

. . . .

Snack: _____

Before Eating   emotion: _____

Hunger rating.......... [   ]

Mind chatter rating..... [   ]

Clarity rating.......... [   ]

After Eating   emotion: _____

Hunger rating.......... [   ]

Mind chatter rating..... [   ]

Clarity rating.......... [   ]

. . . .

Dinner: _____

Before Eating   emotion: _____

Hunger rating.......... [   ]

Mind chatter rating..... [   ]

Clarity rating.......... [   ]

After Eating   emotion: _____

Hunger rating.......... [   ]

Mind chatter rating..... [   ]

Clarity rating.......... [   ]

. . . .

Reflection:

_____

_____

_____

_____

_____

_____

_____

_____

DAY 4

. . . .

Breakfast: _____

_____

Before Eating   emotion: _____

Hunger rating.......... [   ]   _____

Mind chatter rating..... [   ]   _____

Clarity rating.......... [   ]   _____

After Eating   emotion: _____

Hunger rating.......... [   ]   _____

Mind chatter rating..... [   ]   _____

Clarity rating.......... [   ]   _____

. . . .

Snack: _____

_____

Before Eating   emotion: _____

Hunger rating.......... [   ]   _____

Mind chatter rating..... [   ]   _____

Clarity rating.......... [   ]   _____

After Eating   emotion: _____

Hunger rating.......... [   ]   _____

Mind chatter rating..... [   ]   _____

Clarity rating.......... [   ]   _____

. . . .

Lunch: _____

_____

Before Eating   emotion: _____

Hunger rating.......... [   ]   _____

Mind chatter rating..... [   ]   _____

Clarity rating.......... [   ]   _____

After Eating   emotion: _____

Hunger rating.......... [   ]   _____

Mind chatter rating..... [   ]   _____

Clarity rating.......... [   ]   _____

Snack: _____

Before Eating   emotion: _____
Hunger rating.......... [   ]
Mind chatter rating..... [   ]
Clarity rating.......... [   ]

After Eating   emotion: _____
Hunger rating.......... [   ]
Mind chatter rating..... [   ]
Clarity rating.......... [   ]

Dinner: _____

Before Eating   emotion: _____
Hunger rating.......... [   ]
Mind chatter rating..... [   ]
Clarity rating.......... [   ]

After Eating   emotion: _____
Hunger rating.......... [   ]
Mind chatter rating..... [   ]
Clarity rating.......... [   ]

Reflection:

_____
_____
_____
_____
_____
_____
_____
_____

DAY 5

Breakfast: _____

Before Eating   emotion: _____

Hunger rating.......... [   ] _____
Mind chatter rating..... [   ] _____
Clarity rating.......... [   ] _____

After Eating   emotion: _____

Hunger rating.......... [   ] _____
Mind chatter rating..... [   ] _____
Clarity rating.......... [   ] _____

Snack: _____

Before Eating   emotion: _____

Hunger rating.......... [   ] _____
Mind chatter rating..... [   ] _____
Clarity rating.......... [   ] _____

After Eating   emotion: _____

Hunger rating.......... [   ] _____
Mind chatter rating..... [   ] _____
Clarity rating.......... [   ] _____

Lunch: _____

Before Eating   emotion: _____

Hunger rating.......... [   ] _____
Mind chatter rating..... [   ] _____
Clarity rating.......... [   ] _____

After Eating   emotion: _____

Hunger rating.......... [   ] _____
Mind chatter rating..... [   ] _____
Clarity rating.......... [   ] _____

DAY 6

Snack: _____

_____

Before Eating   emotion: _____
Hunger rating.......... [   ]
Mind chatter rating..... [   ]
Clarity rating.......... [   ]

After Eating   emotion: _____
Hunger rating.......... [   ]
Mind chatter rating..... [   ]
Clarity rating.......... [   ]

. . . .

Dinner: _____

_____

Before Eating   emotion: _____
Hunger rating.......... [   ]
Mind chatter rating..... [   ]
Clarity rating.......... [   ]

After Eating   emotion: _____
Hunger rating.......... [   ]
Mind chatter rating..... [   ]
Clarity rating.......... [   ]

. . . .

Reflection: _____

_____

_____

_____

_____

_____

_____

_____

DAY 6

Breakfast: _____

Before Eating   emotion: _____
Hunger rating.......... [   ]
Mind chatter rating..... [   ]
Clarity rating.......... [   ]

After Eating   emotion: _____
Hunger rating.......... [   ]
Mind chatter rating..... [   ]
Clarity rating.......... [   ]

Snack: _____

Before Eating   emotion: _____
Hunger rating.......... [   ]
Mind chatter rating..... [   ]
Clarity rating.......... [   ]

After Eating   emotion: _____
Hunger rating.......... [   ]
Mind chatter rating..... [   ]
Clarity rating.......... [   ]

Lunch: _____

Before Eating   emotion: _____
Hunger rating.......... [   ]
Mind chatter rating..... [   ]
Clarity rating.......... [   ]

After Eating   emotion: _____
Hunger rating.......... [   ]
Mind chatter rating..... [   ]
Clarity rating.......... [   ]

··

Snack: _____

_____

Before Eating   emotion: _____
Hunger rating.......... [   ]
Mind chatter rating..... [   ]
Clarity rating.......... [   ]

After Eating   emotion: _____
Hunger rating.......... [   ]
Mind chatter rating..... [   ]
Clarity rating.......... [   ]

··

Dinner: _____

_____

Before Eating   emotion: _____
Hunger rating.......... [   ]
Mind chatter rating..... [   ]
Clarity rating.......... [   ]

After Eating   emotion: _____
Hunger rating.......... [   ]
Mind chatter rating..... [   ]
Clarity rating.......... [   ]

··

Reflection:

_____

_____

_____

_____

_____

_____

_____

_____

DAY 7

. . . .

Breakfast: _____

_____

Before Eating   emotion: _____
Hunger rating.......... [   ] _____
Mind chatter rating..... [   ] _____
Clarity rating.......... [   ] _____

After Eating   emotion: _____
Hunger rating.......... [   ] _____
Mind chatter rating..... [   ] _____
Clarity rating.......... [   ] _____

. . . .

Snack: _____

Before Eating   emotion: _____
Hunger rating.......... [   ] _____
Mind chatter rating..... [   ] _____
Clarity rating.......... [   ] _____

After Eating   emotion: _____
Hunger rating.......... [   ] _____
Mind chatter rating..... [   ] _____
Clarity rating.......... [   ] _____

. . . .

Lunch: _____

_____

Before Eating   emotion: _____
Hunger rating.......... [   ] _____
Mind chatter rating..... [   ] _____
Clarity rating.......... [   ] _____

After Eating   emotion: _____
Hunger rating.......... [   ] _____
Mind chatter rating..... [   ] _____
Clarity rating.......... [   ] _____

Snack: _____

Before Eating   emotion: _____
Hunger rating.......... [   ]
Mind chatter rating..... [   ]
Clarity rating.......... [   ]

After Eating   emotion: _____
Hunger rating.......... [   ]
Mind chatter rating..... [   ]
Clarity rating.......... [   ]

Dinner: _____

Before Eating   emotion: _____
Hunger rating.......... [   ]
Mind chatter rating..... [   ]
Clarity rating.......... [   ]

After Eating   emotion: _____
Hunger rating.......... [   ]
Mind chatter rating..... [   ]
Clarity rating.......... [   ]

Reflection:

_____

_____

_____

_____

_____

_____

_____

_____

DAY 8

....

Breakfast: _____

Before Eating   emotion: _____
Hunger rating.......... [   ]   _____
Mind chatter rating..... [   ]   _____
Clarity rating.......... [   ]   _____

After Eating   emotion: _____
Hunger rating.......... [   ]   _____
Mind chatter rating..... [   ]   _____
Clarity rating.......... [   ]   _____

....

Snack: _____

Before Eating   emotion: _____
Hunger rating.......... [   ]   _____
Mind chatter rating..... [   ]   _____
Clarity rating.......... [   ]   _____

After Eating   emotion: _____
Hunger rating.......... [   ]   _____
Mind chatter rating..... [   ]   _____
Clarity rating.......... [   ]   _____

....

Lunch: _____

Before Eating   emotion: _____
Hunger rating.......... [   ]   _____
Mind chatter rating..... [   ]   _____
Clarity rating.......... [   ]   _____

After Eating   emotion: _____
Hunger rating.......... [   ]   _____
Mind chatter rating..... [   ]   _____
Clarity rating.......... [   ]   _____

Snack: _____

_____

Before Eating   emotion: _____

Hunger rating.......... [   ]   _____

Mind chatter rating..... [   ]   _____

Clarity rating.......... [   ]   _____

After Eating   emotion: _____

Hunger rating.......... [   ]   _____

Mind chatter rating..... [   ]   _____

Clarity rating.......... [   ]   _____

Dinner: _____

_____

Before Eating   emotion: _____

Hunger rating.......... [   ]   _____

Mind chatter rating..... [   ]   _____

Clarity rating.......... [   ]   _____

After Eating   emotion: _____

Hunger rating.......... [   ]   _____

Mind chatter rating..... [   ]   _____

Clarity rating.......... [   ]   _____

Reflection:

_____

_____

_____

_____

_____

_____

_____

_____

_____

DAY 9

. . . .

Breakfast: _____

_____

Before Eating   emotion: _____
Hunger rating.......... [   ]   _____
Mind chatter rating..... [   ]   _____
Clarity rating.......... [   ]   _____

After Eating   emotion: _____
Hunger rating.......... [   ]   _____
Mind chatter rating..... [   ]   _____
Clarity rating.......... [   ]   _____

. . . .

Snack: _____

_____

Before Eating   emotion: _____
Hunger rating.......... [   ]   _____
Mind chatter rating..... [   ]   _____
Clarity rating.......... [   ]   _____

After Eating   emotion: _____
Hunger rating.......... [   ]   _____
Mind chatter rating..... [   ]   _____
Clarity rating.......... [   ]   _____

. . . .

Lunch: _____

_____

Before Eating   emotion: _____
Hunger rating.......... [   ]   _____
Mind chatter rating..... [   ]   _____
Clarity rating.......... [   ]   _____

After Eating   emotion: _____
Hunger rating.......... [   ]   _____
Mind chatter rating..... [   ]   _____
Clarity rating.......... [   ]   _____

. . . .

Snack: _____

Before Eating   emotion: _____
Hunger rating.......... [   ]
Mind chatter rating..... [   ]
Clarity rating.......... [   ]

After Eating   emotion: _____
Hunger rating.......... [   ]
Mind chatter rating..... [   ]
Clarity rating.......... [   ]

. . . .

Dinner: _____

Before Eating   emotion: _____
Hunger rating.......... [   ]
Mind chatter rating..... [   ]
Clarity rating.......... [   ]

After Eating   emotion: _____
Hunger rating.......... [   ]
Mind chatter rating..... [   ]
Clarity rating.......... [   ]

. . . .

Reflection:

_____
_____
_____
_____
_____
_____
_____

DAY 10

. . . .

Breakfast: _____

_____

Before Eating _____ emotion: _____
Hunger rating.......... [   ]   _____
Mind chatter rating..... [   ]   _____
Clarity rating.......... [   ]   _____

After Eating _____ emotion: _____
Hunger rating.......... [   ]   _____
Mind chatter rating..... [   ]   _____
Clarity rating.......... [   ]   _____

. . . .

Snack: _____

_____

Before Eating _____ emotion: _____
Hunger rating.......... [   ]   _____
Mind chatter rating..... [   ]   _____
Clarity rating.......... [   ]   _____

After Eating _____ emotion: _____
Hunger rating.......... [   ]   _____
Mind chatter rating..... [   ]   _____
Clarity rating.......... [   ]   _____

. . . .

Lunch: _____

_____

Before Eating _____ emotion: _____
Hunger rating.......... [   ]   _____
Mind chatter rating..... [   ]   _____
Clarity rating.......... [   ]   _____

After Eating _____ emotion: _____
Hunger rating.......... [   ]   _____
Mind chatter rating..... [   ]   _____
Clarity rating.......... [   ]   _____

....

Snack: _____

Before Eating   emotion: _____
Hunger rating.......... [   ]   _____
Mind chatter rating..... [   ]   _____
Clarity rating.......... [   ]   _____

After Eating   emotion: _____
Hunger rating.......... [   ]   _____
Mind chatter rating..... [   ]   _____
Clarity rating.......... [   ]   _____

....

Dinner: _____

Before Eating   emotion: _____
Hunger rating.......... [   ]   _____
Mind chatter rating..... [   ]   _____
Clarity rating.......... [   ]   _____

After Eating   emotion: _____
Hunger rating.......... [   ]   _____
Mind chatter rating..... [   ]   _____
Clarity rating.......... [   ]   _____

....

Reflection:

_____
_____
_____
_____
_____
_____
_____
_____
_____

Chapter 10

THE HEADSPACE HANDY GUIDE TO NUTRITION

THE BASICS

Do you remember that food pyramid that gives a quick and easy guide for all the different types of food we should eat? Maybe some of you even have a copy of it on your fridge door. This pyramid was (and still is by some) seen as a way of standardising general nutritional advice, to limit confusion and encourage healthy eating choices. Things have moved on a little since that pyramid first came out, but much of the advice still holds true. Again, I would like to stress that mindful eating is *not* a prescriptive diet, but in case the thought of following a 10-Day Plan without any nutritional guidance whatsoever is bringing you out in a cold sweat, then here is an adapted version of this food pyramid, which explains all the major food groups and some examples and suggestions for each group.

At Headspace we've chosen (on the good advice and authority of our in-house Dietary Consultant) to combine the basic food groups and nutritional building blocks to create seven distinct groups as follows: Carbohydrates (Starch), Carbohydrates (Sugar), Fat (Healthy), Fat (Unhealthy), Protein, Vegetables and Fruit. Obviously it will depend on your size and weight as to how much of each you need to eat to maintain or reach a healthy weight, so this really should be seen as a very rough guide only. Also (and here comes the obligatory disclaimer), if you are pregnant, breast-feeding, suffering from a medical condition, allergies or intolerances, or are younger than two years old (kudos on your reading ability), you should get medical advice to make sure that your nutritional needs are being fully met. All that said and done, here's how our science boffin breaks it down, in terms of getting the balance of those different food groups, and just a few examples of foods that fit into each category (with some foods obviously crossing over into more than one category):

1. Carbohydrates (Starch):

You can eat a moderate amount of these (portion size recommendations coming up shortly).
Rice, pasta, potato, noodles, pearl barley, bulgar wheat, cous-cous, wholewheat bread, tortillas

2. Vegetables:

You can eat as much as you like of these.
Cabbage, carrots, beetroot, peppers, asparagus, peas, corn, celery, spinach, cucumber

3. Fruit:

Eat a moderate amount of these (they can sometimes be high in natural sugar).

Apples, oranges, kiwi, blueberries, bananas, grapes, cherries, raspberries, apricots, plums

4. Protein:
You probably only need 2–3 portions a day of these.
Lean chicken, turkey, red meat*, fish, tofu, eggs**, milk, natural yoghurt, unsalted nuts, beans, chickpeas, lentils

5. Fats (Healthy):
Often neglected, but vital to our health, just a couple of portions a day.
Avocado, olives, oily fish, walnuts, almonds, seeds (pumpkin, sunflower, linseed, flax, etc.)

6. Carbohydrates (Sugar):
Eat at your own risk, fully understanding the consequences.
Ice cream, confectionery, poor-quality chocolate, biscuits, jam, syrup, fizzy drinks

7. Fats (Unhealthy):
If you're looking to get in shape, then these aren't going to help.
Butter, cheese, cream, margarine, mayonnaise, vegetable oil, biscuits, cakes, crisps

---

* *We would recommend a maximum of three portions of red meat a week.*
** *Although they are an excellent source of protein, the egg yolk is quite high in fat. That doesn't mean it's bad for you, but we suggest no more than one egg a day, maximum.*

A QUICK WORD ON CARBOHYDRATES

Now I know that for some people the idea of including *any* kind of carbohydrates in their diet will be a cause of both confusion and terror, but hear me out. The first thing to remember is that this is not a diet, in which you can exclude certain food groups without suffering any side effects. Nor is it a temporary fix where you can stave off the boredom of eating the same foods every day by promising yourself that the end of the diet is in sight. This is a new way of eating, for the rest of your life, and so excluding foods like this is neither helpful, practical or healthy. More than that, however, there is so much misunderstanding about carbohydrates.

First off, there are two types of carbohydrates – the starchy variety and the sugary variety. It is the former that I am recommending on a daily basis, but a small amount of the latter every once in a while won't do you any great harm either. Now, although the starchy carbohydrates are all lumped together in one group, they are not necessarily equal. You've probably already heard of the Glycaemic Index (GI), which gives a score to carbohydrates based on the amount of 'simple sugars' they contain. What this means is that a waffle, which has quite a high GI score, will release sugars (the energy from the food) into your bloodstream relatively quickly, whereas a portion of wholegrain rice, which has a much lower GI score, will take longer to release its energy into your bloodstream.

Because of this, high GI foods tend to lead to a 'blood-sugar peak', followed quickly by a 'blood-sugar trough'. It is this 'crash' that can leave you feeling a little lethargic and sleepy – and arguably more likely to snack on something sweet to 'pick you up'. On the other hand, low GI foods help to maintain a stable blood-sugar level, which leaves you feeling more balanced and less likely to snack on unhealthy food. So, the general guidance is that when you're choosing your starchy carbohydrates, aim for the ones with the lowest GI scores. Here are some examples, with an approximate score next to each one, to give you some idea of how the scale works.

Examples of GI Ratings

Asparagus (10), Tomatoes (15), Pearl barley (25), Soy milk (30), Apple (35), Spaghetti (40), Macaroni (45), Oatmeal (50), Brown rice (55), Bran muffin (60), Raisins (65), Processed white bread (70), French fries (75), Jelly Beans (80), Cornflakes (85), Processed instant rice (90), Dried dates (100).

Whatever you do, though, please don't mindlessly follow the herd and avoid carbohydrates altogether. They are one of the essential building blocks for good health and are needed by the body. There are countries in the world whose people eat little else but natural carbohydrates, and yet who tend not to be overweight at all. It all depends on what you eat, how much you eat of it, and what you add to it. Will lots of dough-nuts make you fat? Quite possibly. Will lots of wholegrain rice make you fat? Absolutely not. Of course, if you add pork chops, melted cheese and a rich creamy sauce to that same rice every time, then the equation changes. Likewise, good-quality bread is very unlikely to make you fat. But add lashings of butter and jam to it every time and eat it throughout the day and night, then things begin to look a little different. If you want to cut out the sugary, processed, refined carbohydrates, then please be my guest. But whatever you do, don't quit the natural, healthy, low GI forms of starchy carbohydrates that will ultimately help you to reach your ideal shape, weight and size.

VITAMINS AND MINERALS – THE MISSING INGREDIENT

Now you may well have expected to see vitamins and minerals included in the main food groups, but the truth is, as long as you are eating a well-rounded diet, with plenty of fresh fruits, vegetables and natural foods, then you will most probably be getting all of the essential vitamins and minerals that you need. There can also be a tendency, once we get into the nitty-gritty of nutrition, to veer towards over-thinking things: 'Am I eating enough Vitamin A . . . what are my calcium levels at the moment . . . do I need to up my intake of Folic Acid?' Remember, mindful eating offers you the opportunity to let go of this type of obsessive thinking (without being irresponsible of course). But in case you're unsure, or even a little curious, then here is a quick round-up of the most important vitamins and minerals, where you can find them, and some of the good things that they will do for you when consumed in healthy amounts.

Vitamins

Vitamin C: Great for keeping your immune system healthy, and for absorbing iron.
Citrus fruits, tomatoes, strawberries, potatoes, broccoli, cabbage

Vitamin B1: This one helps you to produce energy for everyday life.
Meat, wholegrain cereals, milk, beans

Niacin: A serious point of interest, assisting in the breakdown of fats.
Peanut butter, wholegrain cereals, greens, meat, poultry, fish

Vitamin B6: Another cog in the wheel for energy production.
Wholegrain cereals, bananas, meat, spinach, cabbage, lima beans

Folacin: Vital for the regeneration of new cells throughout the body.
Greens, mushrooms, liver

Vitamin B12: Look a little rosier; this one helps to produce red blood cells.
Animal foods (ie. meats and food made from animal products, including dairy)

Vitamin A: Great for your eyes, and even better for your skin.
Milk, egg yolk, liver, yoghurt, carrots, greens, apricots

Vitamin D: Helps with the absorption of calcium, keeping those bones super strong.
Sunlight, fortified dairy products, eggs, fish

Vitamin E: This one is a precious antioxidant, a multitasker.
Vegetable oils, margarine, grains

Vitamin K: Much better than a plaster, this one helps with blood clotting.
Greens, liver

Minerals

Potassium: Keeping those muscles moving, it's vital for exercise.
Apricots, cantaloupe, potatoes, nuts, meats and proteins

Calcium: Looking after the bones and joints, it keeps us moving.
Dairy, salmon, almonds, greens, calcium-fortified foods, soy beans

Folic acid: What *doesn't* it do? Especially important for pregnant mums and little ones.
Spinach, lentils, asparagus

Copper: It's not just good for your blood, it also helps to produce energy.
Kiwi, lima beans, most proteins, most nuts, most beans

Iron: Say goodbye to anaemia, this one is all about producing more red blood cells.
Raisins, beef, sardines, most nuts, green beans, butternut squash, apricots

Iodine: Keeping your base metabolic rate in check, this one is vital.
Fruits, nuts and vegetables grown in iodine-rich soil

Magnesium: Bringing some much-needed calm and relaxation into your life.
Avocado, artichoke, peas, nuts, most legumes

Manganese: This one helps to keep your blood-sugar levels stable.

Banana, kale, buckwheat, egg, most legumes

Phosphorous: Is all about growth and renewal of tissue cells.

Dates, pumpkin, Brazil nuts, oats, tuna, most legumes

Selenium: Another precious antioxidant, protecting the body against free radicals.

Passion fruit, Brussels sprouts, rye, meats and proteins

Zinc: Helps you stay fighting fit and looking your best – great for the skin.

Pomegranate, asparagus, pumpkin seeds, meats and proteins, most legumes

This is just a brief overview, but hopefully the nutritional information in this chapter will give you a greater degree of confidence in selecting the foods that will best help you achieve your aims and ambitions, and which will best enable you to stay fit and well. Just to help you remember it all, I've put together the mindful eating Top 10. This brings together many of the important highlights from this chapter and also provides a few more essential hints and tips for establishing positive, sustainable change in your eating habits. These are not rules, but simply information and guidance that, when incorporated into your life, will assist you in finding a place of outer satisfaction and inner contentment.

THE MINDFUL EATING NUTRITION TOP 10

1. Choose natural foods that are unprocessed and unrefined whenever possible . . .

And if they are also free from any additives, preservatives, any other artificial stuff, then that's even better.

Tip: Watch out for hidden salts, sugars, fats and E numbers!

2. Choose rich, dark or bright-coloured fruit and vegetables whenever possible.

These typically contain lots of good nutrients and are rich in vitamins and minerals. Try to eat more vegetables than fruit and avoid overcooking them too.

Tip: Watch out for pre-prepared bags of vegetables: they can have less nutritional value!

3. Choose starchy carbohydrates that have a low GI score whenever possible.

This will not only help to regulate your calorie intake (without you having to think about it), but it will also help to prevent those sugar highs and lows that result in snacking.

Tip: Watch out for processed varieties of food, which have a higher GI score!

4. Choose protein-based foods that are lean and healthy whenever possible.

It might be a case of finding a leaner cut of meat,

replacing meat with fish once in a while, or choosing one of the many plant-based protein options out there instead.

Tip: Watch out for visible fat on meat and cut it off before cooking!

5. **Choose unsaturated, plant-based fats whenever possible.**
Not all fats are equal and many people make the mistake of trying to eliminate them from their diet altogether. But some fats are essential. Just make sure you get the right type.

Tip: Watch out for those salad dressings, sauces and spreads!

6. **Choose regular full-fat foods rather than low-fat varieties whenever possible.**
Foods designed for weight loss are often so lacking in taste once the fat has been removed, that the only way of making them edible is adding lots of sugar and additives.

Tip: Watch out for packaging that screams 'low fat'. Low fat does not mean low calorie!

7. **Choose to opt out of the sugar-rush whenever possible.**
Whilst enjoying something sweet every now and then is one of the true pleasures in life, consumed in large quantities and on a regular basis, sugar leads to all kinds of problems.

Tip: Watch out for jams, processed honey, sugary cereals, sweet coffees and teas!

8. Choose to avoid foods high in salt whenever possible.

This doesn't just mean not adding salt to your food, but also learning how much commercially prepared foods – such as breads, nuts, crisps, smoked foods, sauces and the like – contain.

Tip: Watch out for the hidden salt in high-street sandwiches!

9. Choose to drink plenty of water on a daily basis whenever possible.

There's no need to carry a water bottle around with you, but try to consume about two litres a day if you can. This can also come from fruit or herbal teas.

Tip: Watch out for heavy coffee consumption, which can adversely affect the body!

10.Choose to eat a diet that is varied and even seasonal whenever possible.

We need a diet that is rich in variety to provide all the necessary vitamins and minerals, and to keep us feeling motivated about food and to reduce the risk of intolerances developing.

Tip: Watch out for old routines. Rotate grains, meats, fish, fruit and vegetables regularly!

* Oh, and one extra note for those of you who might consume more alcohol than is generally recommended . . . Remember that it's not just what it's doing to your liver (or your mind), but also to your waistline. Most alcohol is also very high in sugar, which provides the body with lots of excess calories, but with no nutritional value.

PORTION SIZES

It would be impossible to sign off this chapter on nutritional advice without at least mentioning portion size. Because, although it doesn't fit very neatly into the blame game culture that this society has developed towards food, there is a certain school of thought that would seem to suggest that no food is inherently bad for you – it is only how you choose to consume it, and how much of it you choose to consume that creates the potential for harm. This is an interesting idea and within the framework of mindful eating is a very important distinction to make. However, it also brings portion size under the spotlight. There is no doubt that the increasingly common tendency to 'supersize' portions is having a drastic impact on the number of overweight and obese individuals in the world. So, how much is too much?

Well, if you were to follow the general recommended guideline for eating, the different portion sizes would look something like this:

Carbohydrates (Starch)
1 portion = 1 slice bread, 1/2 cup of cooked rice or pasta, or 30g of ready-to-eat cereal

Vegetables

1 portion = 1/2 cup of raw carrots, 1 cup of raw cabbage, or 1/2 cup of fresh tomato

Fruit

1 portion = 1 slice of fresh melon, 1/2 cup canned fruit, or 1/4 cup of dried fruit

Protein

1 portion = 70–85g cooked lean meat, poultry or fish, 1/2 cup cooked beans, or 1 egg

Fats (Healthy)

1 portion = 1/8 of an avocado, 1 teaspoon of olive oil, or 30g of almonds

Carbohydrates (Sugar)

1 portion = 1/2 cup of raisins, 1 large fresh fig, or 4 teaspoons of jam

Fats (Unhealthy)

1 portion = 1 teaspoon of butter, 1 tablespoon of mayo, or 30g of hard cheese

Now I don't know about you, but I always find these figures quite sobering, because the portion sizes are far, far smaller than those I usually see served up. I don't know anyone who sticks to these serving sizes. And I didn't even touch on the minuscule serving suggestions for ice cream, doughnuts or chocolate (you can imagine what those are). Once again, exactly how much you will need to consume will depend on a whole host of factors, including your weight, your lifestyle, the amount of activity you do, your age, your body type – not to mention your weight-loss goals. But nonetheless, it's interesting to put your own portion sizes into context and see how they might differ somewhat from the official recommendations. Of course, it's fine to indulge once in a while. Some would even say that it is healthy to. But always remember the simple equation that if 'energy in' exceeds 'energy out', then that energy has to go somewhere. And, as you well know, it's favourite hiding place is usually somewhere around your stomach or rear end.

So, why do you serve up, or choose to order, the portion sizes that you do? There's been a huge amount of research in this area over the past few decades, and scientists have come up with some interesting discoveries. For example, in one study when burgers were reduced in size, people immediately noticed and said they still felt hungry after eating. But when those burgers were packed out with extra salad and not squashed down, people said they felt full. This is despite the fact that they were consuming a few hundred calories *less*. In another study, additional air was whipped into half of a smoothie mix, doubling its volume. People who drank that particular smoothie not only ate less food with their lunch, but also reported feeling fuller much sooner. One of my favourite studies is the popcorn experiment, which has been carried out by many research labs around the world. In this experiment, one group of people are given regular tubs of popcorn, whereas others are given supersize portions. Usually both groups have had the same lunch or dinner beforehand to level the playing field. Unsurprisingly, those who have the larger serving size nearly always consume more popcorn. But in some studies this has averaged out at over 50 per cent more, despite the fact that they reported the same level of hunger and relative fullness beforehand. This all seems to suggest that if it's on the plate, we'll eat it.

Only you can decide what is an appropriate size portion. Many studies have found that by reducing portion sizes by just 20 per cent, the body seems to be unable to even register the difference, and so doesn't kick up any fuss at all. Give it a go and see what happens. Here are my favourite tips for establishing and maintaining healthy portion sizes, within the context of mindful eating.

THE HEADSPACE GUIDE TO PORTION SIZES

1. Listen to your body

Before you serve up a mountain of food on your plate, or break open the family size bag of crisps, take a moment to listen to your physical needs. Are you hungry? And if you are, how hungry are you? Dish out just enough food to satisfy the hunger of the body, rather than trying to quench the limitless desire of the mind. You'll be much less likely to go back for more than if you simply had the pack of crisps sitting on your lap.

2. Use smaller serving plates and bowls

Studies have shown that our satisfaction is tied in to 'relative' portion sizes. So, if we have a very small plate that is piled high with food, we will feel much more satisfied than if we have a large plate with a small amount of food

– even if the large serving on the small plate contains less! Some new crockery could be the best investment you've ever made.

3. Be flexible when eating out

Food menus are generally written in a way that encourage you to eat as much as possible while at the restaurant (and why wouldn't they?). But you don't have to play their game. There is no obligation to have a starter, main and dessert. Why not have a starter *instead* of the main course? And why not have a tea or coffee instead of dessert for a change? Oh, and don't be afraid to ask for excess food to be put in a doggie-bag.

4. Serve up at source

When serving up food at home, try to plate it up by the oven or hob, rather than at the table. If the excess is on the table in front of you whilst you're eating, then that's where your mind is likely to be. In fact, studies have also shown you are likely to eat faster with the excess in front of you. Presumably this is prompted by some survival instinct from the past, when we weren't sure where the next meal was coming from.

5. When you eat, just eat

Portion sizes are intimately related to 'how' we eat. For example, if you sat down at a table with a large box of chocolates and no distractions, I am quite sure you would not polish off the entire box. This is partly because you would be more aware of hunger levels, but also because you would probably feel greedy, embarrassed or ashamed. But when you're watching TV, surfing the net, or involved in some other activity, this awareness can get drowned out.

6. Learn what a portion size is

If you're looking to become more mindful of portion sizes, and possibly even to follow the recommended quantities with certain foods, it can be really useful to know and understand what portion sizes are (which incidentally are quite different to 'serving sizes', which can be frighteningly large). As a general rule, a 'cup' is about the size of a large tennis ball or baseball, 85g of meat is about the size of a deck of cards, and 30g of cheese is about the size of domino. Knowing this will hopefully avoid you having to weigh everything.

7. Think 'little and often'

Many people overeat at meals because they are worried they might feel hungry later on. But the body doesn't really work like this and all that tends to do is increase the dramatic swings in blood-sugar levels that will, in all likelihood, see you reaching for the biscuit tin. Try to maintain a stable blood-sugar level and a moderate level of satiety by eating small meals throughout the day (as recommended in the 10-Day Plan) rather than just a couple of ridiculously large meals.

8. Have a salad as a starter

We often dive into large portions of rich and calorie-dense foods simply because we're hungry. The truth is, in these situations, we're often so hungry that we'd eat just about anything. So be smart, eat some raw vegetables or salad to burn off that extreme hunger before the meal itself; that way you will not feel the same need to overindulge in the richer tasting foods.

9. Have a glass of water before eating

The sensation of thirst is often confused with the feeling of hunger, meaning that whenever we feel thirsty, we tend to reach out for a snack. Or, if we're about to serve up a meal, we're likely to put more food on the plate. To ensure that you are listening to the right signals, sip a good-sized glass of water in the 10 to 15 minutes leading up to a meal. This way you can be sure that you are serving up only what the body actually needs.

10.Shop smart

Bulk-buying foods can often enable you to pick up some great bargains and get much better value for money. But know your own mind. If you are unable (or unwilling) to break those down into smaller portion sizes when you get home, then consider the possibility of buying smaller versions. Whilst you may not get the same value for money, take a moment to think of the cost (financial, physical, mental and emotional) of overeating large portions of food.

Chapter 11

MINDFUL EATING AS A WAY OF LIFE

Inherent to the practice of mindful eating, and the broader concept of mindfulness in everyday life, is the understanding of change. Mindfulness reminds us that change is possible, no matter who we are, what we look like, and what our current situation might be. It reminds us that if we can only learn to be present, aware of the potential in each and every moment, then we have the extraordinary opportunity to direct that change towards a healthier and happier way of life. This is a change based on our core values and our true aspirations, rather than a fleeting emotion or habitual thought. It is a change that facilitates better physical health, greater peace of mind, and a profound sense of ease with who we are, what we eat, and how we look. This is mindful eating, and this is what it means to get in shape, to stay in shape, for good.

Mindful eating is unquestionably a new way of *eating*, it is also a new way of *living, feeling* and *being*. It is not something temporary, to get you into an outfit for a party next week (although you may well find that happens anyway), but rather a sustained, practical and manageable way of looking your best, and feeling your best every day. This means at last saying goodbye to the fads and fashions that encourage yo-yo dieting, saying goodbye to calorie counting, weighing yourself, and endlessly thinking about food the whole time. And it also means saying goodbye to the critical and judgemental voice in your head that is never quite satisfied with how you look. In exchange, now is the time to say hello to lasting health and happiness, and to feel good about how you look.

The beauty of mindful eating on *The Headspace Diet* is that it shows you how to develop a sense of happiness, ease and satisfaction *at the same time* as getting in shape, so that reaching your ideal weight will feel effortless compared to previous, temporary diets. Dare I say it might even be enjoyable? It will also mean that the decisions you make will be based on clearly defined ideas, rather than the roller-coaster of emotional instability. And because of this, it will get you to where you want to go.

Mindful eating is about letting go of blame, and reclaiming your responsibility for choice, decision-making and the consequences. By sitting to do Take10 each day, you will be familiarising yourself with what it means to be present, what it means to have a calm mind, and what it means to see thoughts and feelings with clarity. You will then be that much better equipped to apply the same calm and clarity of mind to selecting, shopping, preparing, cooking and eating the foods you enjoy. Remember, the Headspace website (www.headspace.com) is an amazing resource for learning this skill and is entirely free to use over the course of the 10 days – all you need to do is register. If you are feeling inspired and want to learn more, then you can do that too. Whatever you do though, please don't underestimate the importance of this mind training technique.

As I said in the Introduction, mindfulness has been around for thousands of years, and mindful eating for almost as long. It has survived for such a long time for one simple reason – *it works*; and now modern technology and scientific research are showing us exactly *why it works*. Remember, mindfulness has been shown to reduce thinking (including thoughts about food and the body), reduce the overwhelming intensity and frequency of emotion (including the desire for food and self-loathing towards the body), and also to reduce the incidence and severity of multiple physical symptoms, such as heart disease, high blood pressure, IBS and insomnia. It has even been shown to encourage a gentle, compassionate, and accepting attitude towards oneself. It is hard to imagine another technique that comes with so much authenticity, that promises so much, and which has been shown to deliver so consistently in clinical trials.

This is just the beginning, this is the first 10 days of something incredible, something truly life-changing. But it is just the first 10 days. This is a totally new way of eating, which I sincerely hope you will incorporate into your life on an ongoing basis. And if you do this, it will quickly become second nature. You won't even need to think about it. It will simply be *what you do, how you are, and the way you live*. But it will be more than that too. Because how you choose to live your own life affects those around you. It affects those close to you, family and friends who benefit from your good health, your happy state of mind, and your relaxed and sane approach to eating. But it also affects those much farther away, those who are involved in the cultivation and production of the foods you choose to eat. In this way, mindful eating encourages us to reflect on the wider world, our place within it, and the extraordinarily delicate balance of interdependence that exists. Knowing our place within that world, mindfulness clearly points the direction to a happier and healthier way of life.

Put Andy in your pocket with the Headspace app

It's a course of guided meditation, from the author of this book, Andy Puddicombe. Just search 'headspace meditation' in the App Store, on Google Play or visit **headspace.com**

Best of all, our beginner's course,
Take10, is **completely free.**

 HEADSPACE®

Also by Andy Puddicombe

THE HEADSPACE GUIDE TO . . .
MINDFULNESS AND MEDITATION

'No incense, No religion. And you can do it over lunch.'
New York Times

'The experts' expert. Simplicity is the key with this
technique . . . no mystical mumbo jumbo . . . the Headspace
approach is straight forward and relaxed.'
The Times

Available in Hodder paperback and Ebook
www.hodder.co.uk